FIFTY SHADES OF FUNNY:

Hook-ups, Break-ups And Crack-ups

DC Stanfa & Susan Reinhardt

Dedicated to Patch Rose, the Zuzu's petals of this project.
We keep you in our pockets to remind us that this is a wonderful life!

Apologies and Acknowledgements

We are very sorry if we offend anyone with the title or the contents of this book. We are even sorrier if we don't.

We'd like to apologize to our preachers and understand if you start avoiding us at the church picnic.

We want to also thank God for His or Her infinite sense of irony and humor, and for this real-life sitcom you are writing for us, and for helping us find some of your funniest cowriters. Special thanks also for not giving them that one deadly sin of greed, since we barely paid them, and they knew it ahead of time. Thanks also for our favorite deadly sin, lust, and for giving it to everybody, including Jimmy Carter.

We also want to apologize to our mommas for rediscovering our inner hussies, whom we thought (and they hoped) got kidnapped in 1989. We thank you for still talking to us at the church picnic.

Thanks, in advance to all of the brilliant people who will buy this book—we need the bucks for Botox and cosmetic fillers necessary for proper mid-life maintenance. Our mommas and our mirrors are also grateful. Facelifts are also not out of the question, but first and foremost, giving to wonderful charities helping children and/or animals. Perhaps even the Poor Women Need Happy Toys, Too Foundation.

Special thanks to Sherry Stanfa-Stanley for consulting with us on this project, and Robin O'Bryant and Nikki Knepper for introducing us to some great talent in your blogospheres/friend zones. Much appreciation to our associate editor, Delia Su, for keeping us focused and organizing our disorganization. Additional editing credits go to Lisa Golden and Aimee Heckel. Cori Lynne Stanfa Hedrick (DC's daughter) came up with the cool cover concept. And finally, *Fifty Shades of Gratitude* to all of our contributors. We hope that your participation in this book will serve as a GPS to some truly wonderful places—and perhaps we will someday meet in those places. We're thinking an authors' cruise? Readers and authors, please contact us if you are interested!

DC and Susan

Contents

The Things We Do for Love

by Sher Bailey

I t's funny how things you haven't thought about in years suddenly and unexpectedly show up in your thoughts.

Yesterday, while driving back from a field trip with my son's fourth grade class, I remembered a night some twenty-two years ago that I'm sure I had managed to block out of my conscious mind due to the sheer level of embarrassment it caused. All these years later, I can finally laugh at the memory. At least I think I can.

I was eighteen years old and freshly dumped by the man I thought would be my husband. My grandmother had passed away, and, for the first time in two years, I was between boyfriends. I was depressed and on the prowl for a replacement model (fiancé, not grandmother) when I decided to visit my mother in Ft. Knox, Kentucky.

Ft. Knox is an army base and as such, it is always teeming with young, disciplined, lonely men. Any female with most of her teeth can find a man on a military base. I was gonna get me one.

In 1982, eighteen was old enough to be granted access to the clubs on an army post as well as old enough to drink as long as it was only beer or wine. I was all set to go to the NCO (non-commissioned officers) club that Friday night to hunt for a husband.

I spent the entire day in preparation. In much the same way you wash, wax, and detail a car before you try to sell it, I was making sure my chassis was in mint condition.

I carefully applied vampire-red, insanely long, Lee Press-On Nails. Rather than take any chance that one might pop off and leave me claw-challenged, I decided to go one better than the little sticky tabs that come in the package. I grabbed a bottle of Super Glue…the same kind they used to lift Volkswagens over that man's head in the commercials. If it was tough enough to suspend automobiles in midair, surely it could keep my nails in place.

I twisted open a brand-new tube of Coppertone QT and covered my entire body. I knew that nothing attracts a man like a bright orange glow. I couldn't reach the backs of my shoulders, but I figured it would be dark in the club and men wouldn't be interested in the backs of my shoulders anyway.

I curled and teased my long brown hair for at least two hours in order to achieve heights and widths that would leave any 1972 country music diva envious. Not yet satisfied with the large, winged helmet that was my coif, I bent over at the waist as was customary in my daily hair-fixing ritual and flipped my gigantic head of hair upside down so as to achieve maximum hair volume. I then aimed my industrial-sized bottle of Final Net Ultra Hold hair spray and coated the underside of my hair.

When I could touch my hair without having my fingers or various bugs get stuck in it, or when I was nearly ready to pass out, whichever came first, I stood straight again and started the Final Net process on the rest of my hair.

It was the epitome of big hair. And under no circumstances or weather conditions was it ever, ever going to move. The only thing that could penetrate my giant mass of brown locks was water, and I was praying to the rain gods that the skies remained clear. I knew if even the slightest amount of water touched my masterpiece, my head would turn into a colossal mass of chewing gum. A veritable Roach Motel.

I almost forgot to mention the stunning white and gold headband I was wearing across my forehead, circa "Let's Get Physical." Olivia Newton-John had nothing on me. I was simply fabulous and totally ready for the world to hear my body talk.

I pulled on a lime-green and orange striped shirt with spaghetti straps and a short lime-green skirt that had little metal snaps on the pockets. I wanted to show a lot of skin in order to accentuate my brand new tan-from-a-bottle.

When we arrived at the club, I was reminding myself that, above all else, I needed to appear cool. I certainly looked like an attractive, completely adult woman capable of bearing healthy children and cooking wonderful meals. Now I needed to act the part.

And how better to say to the world, "I am an adult" than to drink to excess and smoke cigarettes? That's what I needed to do. Smoke and drink. My stunning beauty would grab 'em, and smoking and drinking would seal the deal. Screw the surgeon general. He probably didn't own a Crock-Pot, I doubt he was even remotely domestic, and if he had done any decent research, he would have discovered that Final Net was much more deadly to the lungs than Virginia Slims Menthol Lights.

I went to a cigarette machine (they still had such things in 1982) and picked the pack that I thought most reflected my femininity. The Virginia Slims, of course. I found a table near the stage where a very loud band was playing, and tried to act as if I sat in bars every night.

The waitress showed up and asked me what I wanted to drink. This was a toughie. I couldn't just order beer or wine even though the law said that was all I could drink. Sophisticated women like me drank mixed drinks. The only mixed drink for which I could recall a name was 7 & 7, so that's what I ordered. I had no clue what it was, but it sounded like a womanly drink to me.

As I waited for my frou-frou drink to arrive, I noticed that the band featured a scorchingly hot drummer. He was beautiful. He had long, black hair, dark skin, and coal-black eyes. I loved him immediately and imagined how precious our dark-haired children would be. I began trying to make eye contact.

I don't know if it was my high hair, my vampire nails, or the striking contrast of my burnt-orange skin against my lime-green outfit, but he couldn't take his eyes off me. He'd smile and wink and I'd act as if I was way too cool to notice, even though my heart was about to beat out of my chest.

When the band took a break, he made his way to my table and ordered a shot of tequila with a beer back. What a grown-up, manly thing to order! I didn't know what a beer back was, but I found it terribly exciting that the father of my children did.

He told me I was beautiful and wanted to know if I'd like to go with him to another bar when he was through with this gig. How much did I love the fact that he used a word like "gig"! It was going to be so much fun being married to a drummer who drank beer backs and had gigs.

His break was almost over when I realized that I had one bit of ammunition I had not yet used. I hadn't smoked in front of him. Silly girl. He needed to see me smoke in order to get the full effect.

I should probably mention that the only times I had smoked and actually inhaled prior to this moment brought on spontaneous puking that lasted for hours. I figured that as long as I didn't inhale, I'd avoid the never attractive but totally inevitable vomiting. I was so smart, it's no wonder he wanted me.

Trying to open the pack with my nails was like handing it to Edward Scissorhands, but I finally managed to pry it apart and extract one long, thin cigarette. Now I just had to get it in my mouth and light it and I was home free.

I picked up the Bic and noticed that the cigarette felt a little sticky in my hands. Apparently, I had not completely gotten all the hair spray off my fingers.

I clicked the lighter once. Nothing. I clicked it again. Nothing.

When I clicked it the third time I heard a sound not unlike the sound you hear when you turn on a gas stove—*whoosh!*

Warmth spread across my hands. Two of my beautiful red nails were fully engulfed. I was literally on fire.

Had I been at home and my fingers burst into flames, I might have considered stop, drop, and roll. But ever the cool-headed adult, I didn't want to scare off the love of my life by acting like this was a big deal.

I did what any logical person would do when a part of her body is on fire: I held my hand close to my face and gently blew as if my fingers were nothing more than birthday candles. What I failed to take into consideration was that the very same hair spray that was coating my artificial nails and making them as flammable as a BBQ grill was all over my head. That dawned on me about the time my bangs started to smoke.

It was at that moment that "cool" went right out the window (as if it hadn't left the building already). I stuck my flaming hand in my 7 & 7 while frantically beating my forehead with the other one. The fire was finally extinguished.

While I sat there smoldering and smelling of burnt hair and fake nails, with my hand soaking in my drink glass, I asked my super-hot drummer with his gigs and beer backs, "So, what time do you think you'll be done here?"

Sher Bailey *is a nationally recognized and highly sought-after marriage and relationship expert licensed through the Universal Life School of One-Hour Online Experts. In her spare time, she is a professional theoretical tap dancer and fire-baton twirler who strings together various and assorted sentences that delight her tens of readers the world over, both in prison and out.*

Sher has been the recipient of many prestigious and coveted awards for her essays, such as The Daughters of the American Revolution's writing contest in sixth grade for her piece on Thomas Jefferson, in which she had the good sense not to mention Sally Hemings—mainly because she did not yet know about her.

You can read words Sher writes on www.SherBailey.com and www. Momcaster.com. What she lacks in talent she makes up for in mentions of keeping her ex-husband's testicles in Mod Podge-covered mason jars.

Woman-In-A-Box

by Roberta Beach Jacobson

It was in downtown Amsterdam that Ron first saw the woman of his dreams. In a sex shop. Of course. It was love at first sight, or so he claimed. And so it was that my old college pal Ron bought the woman-in-a-box and took her home to share his apartment and his life.

He decided her name was Tiffany, and he treated her like royalty. He sang to her; he wrote her love poetry. Ron didn't seem to mind that his partner was not exactly a living, breathing human. Ron explained that their sex life was "gentle, yet wild." He told me she was special in many ways and I suppose he had a point. I assumed she'd never gripe about PMS or start an argument. Her figure would not resemble a pear as she approached middle age.

Ron probably found every delight in Tiffany, the woman who would never get wrinkles and who would never complain about his mother. Even better, she could take as much *action* as Ron could give. He'd never hear a single "Not tonight, dear" out of her.

"Tiffany is everything I could want," he told me. "What a woman!" He bought the brunette doll-of-a-woman a wardrobe to die for. She was decked out in designer frocks, lovely hats, lacy underthings, uncomfortable-looking pumps. The works.

"Do you think that shade of blue would look right on Tiffany?" Ron asked me one day as we passed a Chanel shop. Though Ron was not a wealthy man, when it came to his woman, money was apparently no object.

Come to think of it, it couldn't be half bad being Tiffany, getting sensual back rubs and foot massages after each bath. Also, Ron swore he was careful not to press hard on her when thrusting from his missionary position, and I know most of my women friends would appreciate such thoughtfulness for comfort during lovemaking. The constant *slap-slap* of a heavy male belly tends to be distracting if not downright uncomfortable.

Ron had few hobbies. He worked his thirty-eight hours a week in an Amsterdam bank, and then he went home to Tiffany. He put ribbons in her hair and kept the volume on the TV low so she wouldn't be disturbed. As if to prove his love, every Saturday, no matter the weather, Ron walked to the florist on the corner and bought Tiffany a white carnation. She was pampered from the moment she entered his life.

Ron bought a queen-size waterbed. "It's a surprise for Tiffany," he told me on the phone. "She usually stays in bed while I'm at work." I had to admit, Ron and Tiffany had so far outlasted every marriage I knew. Maybe he was on to something after all.

Since Tiffany had come into his life, Ron refused to eat in restaurants, fearing that people would stare at them. So for their fifth anniversary, I arrived with a bottle of champagne and Chinese carry-out. I debated getting two or three entrees and decided on three. What the heck.

"Perfect timing. We're fresh out of the bubble bath," Ron announced as I arrived. Tiffany, delicately perched by the window, was dressed to the nines. I felt a little scruffy in my rumpled pantsuit. I hadn't thought to change after work. Ron shook my hand. I waved over at Her Royal Highness Tiffany, never being sure how to address her. I felt no sense of female bonding with her.

"How about that haircut?" asked Ron, beaming. "I did it myself."

I was lost in thought. I couldn't remember the last time I'd been treated to a romantic and leisurely bubble bath. Sighing, I evaluated the hairdo. "Great look, Tiff. I like the shorter cut on you. Very attractive."

Ron chatted away all during our dinner, which meant I didn't need to struggle with any one-way conversations with Tiffany. We each had a plate at the table. As always, Tiffany didn't eat a bite. Ron wolfed down his egg rolls and half the cashew chicken before thinking to pop open the champagne.

"To my Tiffany," he toasted. "I couldn't ask for a more perfect partner. Thank you for these last five years, the happiest of my life."

Who was I to argue? I knew Ron had been miserable with some of his girlfriends. Most of his more serious relationships had lasted only two or three months. One smoked too much, another was hooked on cocaine. Another not only crashed his car and lied about doing it but ran up his credit card to the limit buying presents for her other boyfriends. Most women in his past had pressured him to get married, as he seemed to be the last bachelor in the city. Let's face it, Ron had actually found his fantasy woman (a one-in-a-million chance), and he was treating her right. There seemed to be no limit on how much he could give — or how much Tiffany could take.

Ron had rented a video, and that's how we spent the rest of the anniversary evening, laughing at an old comedy classic. Around midnight, I could see his longing glances in Tiffany's direction, and I took my cue to leave the lovebirds alone.

Because of my having to travel for business, I didn't see much of Ron for a few years. We'd catch up on the phone when we could. I showed up in great style for their eighth anniversary and brought sixteen long-stemmed red roses, eight for each of them.

Ron had never looked happier. A watercolor of Tiffany in an ornate frame hung over the fireplace. I'd known Ron since grade school and never realized he could wield a brush. But there she was, captured in her dark-haired splendor, mouth perpetually open.

"See how love in the soul and a waterbed in the bedroom brings out the best in a man?" he asked me, proud of his painting achievement. "Here's to another year together!" He raised his glass.

I turned toward the ever-silent Tiffany. Though dressed in a short lavender gown that would have been perfect for a night out at the opera, she looked slightly down. Had she lost weight? I tried not to stare at the patch just below her knee.

"Yep, my darling isn't as robust as she used to be," Ron explained. "But who of us is? We age; it's a fact of life. Now she's all doctored up. No problem."

I had my doubts, but the patched old girl still hung around, as if to prove me wrong.

We met up in Ron's living room for the big tenth anniversary, and what a celebration it was. A cheese platter, a selection of fine wines, a huge roast beef with the works. Salad, breads. He had gone all out, sparing no catering expense for the three of us—possibly suspecting this would be the last such celebration. Tiffany's designer clothes no longer fit properly and her rings wouldn't stay on. She was down, way down. Ron realized it and it pained him. I could see it in his eyes.

I visited them occasionally to see how things were going, but Tiffany was a mere wisp of the alluring woman in the painting.

Was it suicide? Nobody can say. One day, not long after their tenth-anniversary bash, when Ron was at the office, Tiffany blew out an open window and soared over the city. Only her stilettos remained behind.

QUICKIE from DC:

I found this story to be as funny as it was disturbing—and maybe just a tad "over-blown." I had to know if it was really true. Roberta told me that Tiffany was a real (doll) and that even though Ron eventually dated human females, he still considers himself a widower...

*Author and humorist **Roberta Beach Jacobson** (http://www. RobertaBeachJacobson.com) is coauthor of the award-winning* Almost Perfect *(Enspirio House, 2008) and* Saying Goodbye *(DreamofThings,*

2010). She has authored, ghostwritten, translated, edited, or contributed to fifty-four nonfiction books published on four continents.

Her humor writing has been anthologized in best-selling series such as Chocolate for Women *(Simon & Schuster),* Cup of Comfort *(Adams Media), and* Chicken Soup for the Soul. *Hundreds of her articles have been published in newspapers and magazines, some syndicated by King Features and the New York Times Syndicate. She is a member of the Authors Guild and the National Society of Newspaper Columnists.*

Sex in the Cemetery

by Susan Reinhardt

What is it about a man taking you to a fine restaurant and buying your little self a lobster tail or a piece of decent fish that makes him think you owe a piece as well? I'm trying to figure out the crustacean/sex connection somehow wired in my husband's brain.

I always know when he hauls my lumpy ass to the Red Lobster (his favorite place, which I call Redneck Lobster), he expects adult entertainment when we get home.

I've yet to understand how a man stuffed with shrimp, salmon, and fried clams could think of anything but lying on the couch in a semi-coma from all that food. Apparently, it doesn't work that way for them. Men could be on their hospice beds, oxygen tube hanging out of their noses with the unclipped hairs, and death's intravenous drip coursing through their bloodstreams and still… the sheet begins to rise.

How can they be as full as ticks on hemophiliacs and still want to row the boat while all you want to do is drop anchor? Preferably in a tub of hot water or in front of the TV watching McDreamy on *Grey's Anatomy*.

After eighteen years of marriage and every excuse in the book for my not wanting to get happy on the Sealy, you'd think my husband could learn to read the clues.

When I want sex, I'll cuddle up next to him or wear bras and panties that match. As it now stands, I don't plan on my underwear matching unless I'm in my coffin. If I die thin, I shall wear a Victoria's Secret set and that's *it*. No other garments.

So why can't my husband figure out that when I go home and put on my scrubs that cost $1.50 from the thrift shop, this screams "Frumpy Woman with Dead Libido: Do Not Resuscitate"?

While I don't want my mama and daddy reading this next passage, since we're proper Southern people (at least *they* are), I feel it's my duty to include it to show how expensive food can morph into a powerful aphrodisiac. I was going to wait until my folks died to share this, but they seem to be hanging tough, so instead I'll write it and tell them I made it all up. (But it's really true.)

My husband and I had gone to Carrabba's Italian Grill (which he thinks is highly overrated and not up to the Redneck Lobster's standards but which I think is absolutely delicious). We then went to the mall to exchange my birthday present, which had started out as an opal bracelet; I'd told him only women with wiggling teeth wear opals, and thus I ended up with a beautiful garnet and diamond bracelet that sparkles and shines and really is glamorous.

"Why didn't you like my opals?" he asked, a dejected look on his face.

"They're fine if you're twelve and haven't had a period or if you're ninety-five and can't remember your name."

"I hope I'm getting sex tonight because this fish cost a fortune and garnets are four times the price of opals," he said, shoveling in some blackened salmon—aka Carrabba's version of Viagra.

"Opals are fine, hon," I said. "Fine, if you are in seventh grade and the first boy you've ever French kissed gets you one for Christmas. They are also OK if you are eighty years old and have one of those wet, waddling necks. Not that there's a thing wrong with wobbling necks or opals. I'm just not one for either."

We finally finished our fish dinners and were deciding how to culminate the big 4-0 birthday. Due to the fish consumption,

I knew sex was 100 percent likely. Crab claws equal blowjob. Lobster means the full Monty. Anything nearing $60 for the tab means whatever his fish-filled arse desires.

"I wanna do something a wee bit kinky," I said, surprising both myself and my husband, who rarely gets action unless it's from someone I don't know about. When you're married with two kids, two careers, and two different shifts, it's hard to fit *it* in, though I can pull an Oscar performance from the mattress if need be.

"So what do you say? Wanna get ultra wild tonight?"

His ears heated up, going from beige to pink to maroon. "What are you up to now?" my ever-skeptical husband asked. One ear was beginning to curdle and smoke.

Going home would mean putting kids to bed and brushing teeth and hearing some major whining and carrying on and then being too tired to even think about the mattress mambo. Plus one never knows what might transpire once the kids are transported from sitter to home.

"Let's just turn in here and do it in the back of the van," I said as we traveled the road toward home, which is also the road that leads to Pleasant Hill Memorial Gardens, a mountaintop burial ground that is absolutely breathtaking. "Whip it over there."

"The cemetery? Are you out of your mind?"

"I'm forty. It's dark. When you're forty and it's dark, it's OK to have sex in a cemetery or anywhere else you choose. It's not like anyone's going to say anything."

He gave it a second's thought, then found a spot on a knoll. One thing led to another until we were in the backseat and my husband had unfastened and hurled the youngest's car seat for more you-know-what room. The Joy Ride thumped and thudded and landed somewhere down the hill near a family mausoleum.

At that point, I tried to remember the rules of the steamy sex guide from *Redbook* and attacked my husband as if I were a teenager with raging hormones.

"Whoa!" he said. "This isn't the Kentucky Derby. I want to keep my teeth for as long as possible."

We went at it for a while, and I couldn't help noticing a headstone with a little red-white-and-blue American flag bobbing up and down in my line of vision. It was hard to concentrate when I kept seeing the flag and the grave and the big old full moon like a disapproving eye.

When it was all over with, and quite fun I might add, I stepped out of the van and into the cold, moony night to at least introduce myself to the fellow underground who kept entering into my peripheral vision during the Act. I stared at the letters etched into granite and Lord help, of all the thousands of graves in that cemetery, there was John Fields Williams III, husband of a beloved former coworker, now dead two years and one month. A coworker in the freakin' Junior League. Meaning mission-ary position only, curtains pulled, covers up to chin, Astroglide almost a given.

"Sorry about that, John," I mumbled and draped myself over his tombstone, my pants unbuckled and my bra AWOL. "Consider this your lucky night, sir. How many corpses get free porn in your condition? By the way, I loved your wife."

I then hopped in the van laughing like some newly middle-aged woman who hadn't been serviced in a month and had finally got her some in a cemetery.

Cemetery sex, people — give it a whirl after a nice seafood din-ner. I guarantee no one's going to kiss and tell.

Epilogue: I'm now fifty and on my second husband. We've had sex every place you can imagine. Not that anyone cares, just putting it out there.

Spoiler Alert: There Aren't Enough Red Pens in the World

by Shauna Glenn

It's not often that I do book reviews, mostly because everyone has opinions about the books they read, so why would anyone want to know what I think? At least that's how I see it. I don't usually read a book based on someone's review or suggestion: what's important is if the title/cover catches my attention. It's a highly advanced, complicated system you wouldn't begin to understand. The world is lucky to have me.

Recently, I deviated from my careful selection process and bought the book *Fifty Shades of Grey* because everyone was talking about it. I think my friend Brittany's exact quote to me was, "OH MY GOD YOU HAVE TO READ IT, IT WILL MAKE YOU WANT TO HAVE SEX WITH EVERYONE." Like *that's* an offer I can refuse.

So the day I found the package from Amazon sitting on my front porch, I sat in my little cozy spot on the sofa and dove in head first.

I will admit something to you right here, right now. The book is sexy, there's no doubt about it. And yes, it does invite some really strong sexual urge-y feeling things in my girlie bits. And yes, I had a hard time putting it down. The dirty parts are really dirty. And I liked it. I'm sorry you have to read this, Dad.

But.

That was only when I strained my brain really hard not to critique the most horribly written book in the history of published works. Seriously, there aren't enough red pens in the entire world to make all the needed corrections. It started with the ridiculous dialogue and then, when I thought there was no way it could get any worse? Holy gross overuse of exclamation points! Oh my god! They run amok!

I have no idea how this book was signed off, as is, by the publisher. My guess is that the editor in charge of "editing" was in the midst of some post-coital coma and couldn't be bothered. (I say "editing" in quotes because clearly it wasn't "edited" by normal "editing" standards, or by anyone who knows anything about "editing," or even a chimpanzee who was taught how to "edit" after he mastered the skill of stacking cups.)

For a book that's set in the USA in the year 2011, there are several matters I take issue with.

One, the main character, Ana, is twenty-one years old and a senior in college; she's well educated. Yet she doesn't have an e-mail address (!!!), or use the Internet (!!!), or own a computer (!!!)...*and doesn't have a cell phone* (!!!). How do you get through college with no computer and no e-mail address? How do your professors communicate with you, for crying out loud? My nine-year-old has an e-mail address. Hell, my cat has an e-mail address, strictly so that I can open up credit cards in his name (He has excellent credit by the way, but that's not important to the story. You know what I'm trying to say here.)

Two, the other main character, Christian, is twenty-seven years old and a billionaire. He's from America, like Ana, but his vocabulary is something out of a Thomas Hardy novel. It's like the author scoured English literature and picked out all the words she felt might impress the reader. And then she inserted the fancy words into impossibly unrealistic dialogue. She has him saying phrases that no West Coast twenty-something Hot Guy would ever say. Ever. Example: There's a scene where he and his brother are sitting in front of the telly watching a "match" between the Texas Rangers and the Seattle Mariners. It's not a match, it's a game—welcome to America, E.L. James.

Three, I'm serious when I tell you that the book is laden—*laden!*—with exclamation points: They're everywhere! They were so noticeable that I started circling them but had to stop because my pen ran out of ink!

Four, the main character has this ongoing conflict with her subconscious and her inner goddess—outside of the conflict she has with the actual "real" characters in the story. It was so chaotic with these two not-real characters (her subconscious and inner goddess) arguing and name calling and even sticking their tongues out at each other that I found myself just skimming over everything that wasn't sex and getting straight to the nitty-gritty. I'm pretty sure that makes me some kind of sexual deviant, but I don't even care. I just want to read about the sex; is that too much to ask?

I'm sorry if I'm ruining the book for you, but people, I'm doing you a favor by giving you the four-one-one. Trust me. I'm not saying not to read it. I'm just saying forget everything you learned in seventh-grade English class. Pretend you're living back in time before modern language was invented. Go back to the days when early man was drawing genitals on the sides of cave walls. Not those cave walls, the actual cave walls. (Clearly, I've been reading too much porn.)

Who wants my copy of *Fifty Shades of Grey*? It's not signed by the author, but I can draw a picture of a naked girl inside the front cover if that makes you happy.

You know that rumor that Southern women are well mannered and slightly submissive? Though ridiculously good looking, **Shauna Glenn** *is neither of those things. In fact she's borderline offensive—the accent just makes it endearing. She is a stellar mother of four children, even though they often forget to give her presents on her birthday and Mother's Day. They did give her lice once, but it's mostly gone now.*

The rare times Shauna is let out of her house, she gives keynote addresses at conferences such as BlogWorld, *or reads from her latest novel,* Relative Insanity, *at book signings. She writes a humor column for* Fort Worth, Texas *magazine and has been featured on* *various websites that she can't remember the names of. Shauna's website is <u>ShaunaGlenn.com</u>; here, she talks about her experiences raising teenagers, and about wine. (The two are related.)*

Her next book, titled, Your Vagina Is Not A Rattlesnake: And Other Things They Don't Teach You At Church Camp, *will probably never get published because it's a collection of true short stories from her childhood and she's afraid her family will never speak to her again if she puts it out there for the world to read.*

Red Hat Sex

by Liz Langley

This story originally appeared on Alternet.org

You've noticed them—groups of older women in regal purple dresses and signature scarlet caps. They are the Red Hat Society, an international group of women dedicated to enjoying their mellow years with a vigor that makes "mellow" seem quaint. Their mission is to have fun, and to achieve this, they get around.

You may have seen them yourself, but I'll bet you've never seen one of them hold up a vibrator and mime like a sword swallower just to make her friends laugh. I have, and it was charming to witness women who'd fit as the fifth Golden Girl mulling over dildos, cracking wise about cock rings, and wondering how those darn pasties stay on.

Right now is my local Red Hat chapter's "Romance Revival," and I've never seen a group of people enjoy themselves more than these ladies did at our neighborhood adult department store.

Fairvilla Mega Store is the kind of sex shop one might expect to find in a bigger city like Miami or New York rather than in little

G-rated Orlando. It's a clean, well-lit place, two stories of bright candor and casual maturity. It feels like a mall store that just happens to sell vibrators, porn videos, and lots and lots of leather. The store's amiability probably makes it easier for the Hatters to be here, though the red wine doesn't hurt, either.

When I arrive, the pink-cheeked ladies are seated around a long table doing a little icebreaking craft called "Mold Your Perfect Penis," as conceived by Fairvilla's Nikki Mier (whose mom is a Red Hatter—hence today's trip). While the women keep busy rubbing a Play-Doh-like substance into cylindrical shapes, Nikki's mom, a sweetly soft-spoken older woman, comes up to say hello. Her name tag says "Inky."

I don't think anything of this; two other tags read "Brownie" and "Princess." Finally, when I notice "Lassie," I'm told that the ladies are using their "porn star" names, that is, their first pets' names. Lassie has a laugh that's explosive and catching. She's made a small red wiener, which would be funny enough, but people keep calling it "Uncle Bob" (a long story, but less perverse than it sounds).

As "Muscles," "Buttons," and "Bounce" keep working away, quips fly through the cacophonous room: "I can't remember; it's been thirty-five years since I had sex!" and "How do you get the wrinkles out of it?" They build their phalluses in "Hulk" green, indigo blue, and multi-colors. Someone drips wine on the Hulk's head: Penis Noir.

What I love about being here with this crowd is their bubbly reminder that sex and silliness aren't exclusive to the young. The Hatters aren't hitting on the staff or anything, but they aren't prudish either. Watching the ladies' eyes light up as they buy lingerie is a sweet reminder to Never Assume—being discreet doesn't mean you don't know what time it is.

Now that the ice isn't just broken but pulverized, the women begin shopping—and breaking the stereotype that older folks are resistant to new technology. Many say they've never been in a store like this before (though at least one has tried catalogs), but they're buying and browsing with abandon. They buy vibrators and photograph one another holding them. "This is going in my scrapbook," someone says. I imagine her at the craft store, framing happy snaps of Dildo Day.

As things wind down, I elbow Lassie in the arm and point out the penis piñata, just to hear that laugh. I ask her what she found most surprising about today's excursion, and she gestures toward the vibrator area. She says she can't picture anyone buying one when they've got the real thing at home. But, I say, not *everyone* has the real thing at home. What if you can't wait? She can't fathom this—how could it be any fun if it isn't with someone you love?

Just when you think you've heard it all, you get an eye-opener from Lassie. I'm so used to hearing about alternative sexualities that her traditionalist take seems more surprising to me than anything in the store.

The Red Hat ladies leave in a cloud of chatter and charm, and I feel genuinely glad to have spent the day with them. They were as much fun as their club philosophy promised. It's true that sexuality is still important when you're older, but camaraderie is, too. And how could a Play-Doh penis be any fun at all without someone you love to laugh at it with?

QUICKIE from Susan:

I once had a dildo, key word here being once. It was huge and purple and rippled, shining with possibilities. I had been looking forward to trying it out, but it seemed my then eight-year-old son and two-year-old daughter discovered it prior to its inaugural mission. When I arrive on the scene, it was clenched between my tiny Pomeranian's choppers.

"What that thing is, Mama?" little tot daughter asked.

"Hmmm. Well, let's see...that would be a...well...a giant's thumb, honey."

I heard my son snickering. He then fell on the floor with his legs in the air, grasping his little belly. His legs whirled like helicopter blades.

"It's not a thumb, you stupid ass," he said, rolling toward the Dildo Dog.

"Don't say "ass," I admonished. "It's fanny. We are Christians here in this house, and we say 'fanny.'"

He sat up and stared at the dog's new toy.

"Can we say 'dildo', too?" he asked.

"I'm certain I have no idea what you're talking about," I said to my third-grade son, "but never use that term again in this household. God has ears, you know."

Some eleven years later, I received a "Trildo" in the mail. This differs from a dildo in that it has three protuberances guaranteed to hit every spot, including the uvula. I swear it looks like a squid with a bunch of tentacles, and I'm scared to death to use it.

I think I'll toss it to my Border Collie.

Liz Langley is the author of <u>Crazy Little Thing: Why Love & Sex Drive Us Mad</u> and <u>Pop Tart: A Fresh-Frosted Sugar Rush Through Our Pre-Packaged Culture</u>. *A freelance writer and columnist for twenty-one years, she has seen her work published in/on about twenty publications, including Salon, Glamour, the Toronto Sun, and the Orlando Weekly. She currently writes a science column for* Alternet. org, <u>Ten Mind-Blowing Discoveries This Week</u>. *She's also been a radio personality, karaoke hostess, and playwright for, well, not quite as long as she's done the other stuff. She loves you from afar.*

I Will Tell You the Title at the End of this Chapter

By DC Stanfa

Stood up again, with not even a phone call. Cynical as I am, I still didn't see it coming; I really thought I'd found The One—not at all like the others, who were less like Ones and more like Zeros. Just think of all the checks I'd written to them, checks with so many zeros. Them with their promises to take care of my needs and me always expecting a crystal-clear future.

Abandoned again, I was alone and uncertain, without clarity or direction. *What is wrong with me? What did I do to drive them away? I'm nice. I'm patient.* But I knew the real answer: Even the new guy could sense my desperation, and that is never appealing. But this one I trusted. For him, I even broke a rule: I paid him in advance. Phil was older and more experienced than the others. Responsible, stable, I thought. We even laughed at each other's jokes. He called me his "mafia princess."

"I'll see you tomorrow morning," Phil had said. It was two thirty in the afternoon, and I knew he wasn't coming. And Shrek, my built-in swimming pool, was turning greener by the minute. The familiar anxiety began tying knots in my stomach.

How in the hell am I going to clear up the algae in time for Cori's birthday party next week? And then it dawned on me: *No wonder women sleep with their pool boys. You have to keep them happy to keep them around. The money just isn't enough.*

I didn't think my fiancé, Tom, would approve, and in reality I couldn't prostitute myself for such a shallow reason.

Tom and I had been dating less than a year when I found "the house." He declined even to come see it, because, he admitted later, "I was afraid I would talk you out of it because it had a pool. It was your decision, and I didn't want to influence it."

Oh, how often I wished he had. It was the house of Band-Aids and Shrek the pool, who was big and green and ate my money. After three decades of falling for the wrong men, I finally found Mr. Right. Unfortunately, I'd fallen for the wrong house.

My daughter and I had been living in the house her father and I had built, but several years after the divorce, I realized we'd have to move to get Cori on a bus line for middle school. Location, location, location. In my case, the priority should have been low maintenance, low maintenance, low maintenance. What was I thinking? The bigger question was what was Susan, my realtor—also my good friend and neighbor—thinking when she introduced us in the first place?

Susan still tells the story about watching me as I tried to mow my lawn for the first—and last—time after my ex moved out. As she tells it, she thought it was funnier than Lucy Ricardo and the conveyor of candy. Susan is the daughter of a plumber; she does her own electrical work.

Susan, who rehabs houses on the side, has seen me dust tables with my shirt sleeve and hire people to change my light bulbs. Maybe that was it—if she sold me this house, she'd get a sale and years of entertainment. As I grew ever more exasperated with an aging house with a pool and hot tub, Susan would have built-in entertainment without having to watch old *I Love Lucy* episodes. She could just come over and watch me wrestle Shrek.

It was love at first sight. I saw pool parties for Cori and her friends. I envisioned romantic hot tub scenes with Tom that came right out of *The Bachelor*. Turns out being a romantic and a water sign are not good enough reasons to think you should own a pool.

I did not see the forest for the trees that needed trimming, and some that would later need to be removed. As my obsession with an in-ground vinyl lined body of water went off the deep end, my first summer of pool love cost me nearly $2,000 for the professional opening and closing, broken pump, chemicals, and anxiety medication I required.

It would take more than a case of shock therapy to cure me (for you non-pool owners that was a pool owner pun). Not that we don't get any enjoyment out of Shrek. It's just that he can be an ogre as easily as he can be Mike Meyers; it all depends on his mood. Shrek may not even be a he. Our friend Justin likens the pool to a bipolar woman, alternately laughing and weeping throughout the season.

Every summer, it was something different, but it was always expensive. I don't know which is worse: a working heater or a broken heater. The first year, when it worked, the propane bill was $300 and the fuel lasted only two weeks. The next year, when it broke, we just shut the damn thing down altogether. The omen should have been when Cori, while adding chemicals to the pool, fell in and broke her leg.

My pool pity party was probably payback for all the pool hopping and other trespassing I did as a teen. Chlorinated karma.

The next year we suffered a hot tub leak and also needed a new $3,500 vinyl liner for Shrek. Then also began the endless saga of the sand filter. Worst of all, we were barely using the pool. Sure, Cori had the annual pool birthday party—late May and one or two more get-togethers each summer that included swimming. Mostly, on hot summer days Cori would watch TV and text while Facebooking. I worked late and would call her, begging her to use the pool. I nagged and played the guilt card: "All the time and money I put into this stupid house and this stupid pool, and you could be living in a prison cell, as long as you have your TV and your laptop. Who did I buy this house for then, anyway?" I sounded like Rose from *Gypsy*. Gypsy answers, "I thought you did it for me, Mama."

The truth is that a pool is like a boat. You don't really want to be an owner—you just want to be friends with an owner. If *b-o-a-t* stands for *Break Out Another Thousand*, (in reference to its expensive maintenance) then I believe p-o-o-l really means *Peel Off One Large*. And it isn't just about the money. It's also the psychological roller coaster, the uncertainty. It's like being under the spell of a fickle lover (or at the mercy of unreliable pool boys).

It was now six p.m. and there had still been no call from Phil, my latest pool boy. I called Tom for support. He'd been through this before with me and felt nearly as frustrated and helpless as I did.

"I thought Phil was the real deal, DC. I can't believe he stood you up. Maybe something happened."

I did a brief déjà vu to my dating years when I was naïve enough to think that, yes, surely something must have happened. In the past, I'd call the guy and start leaving messages. Nice ones at first, like, "I hope you're OK, and did you possibly forget we had plans tonight?" Then hours later, after a bottle of wine, the drunk-dialing: "This better be good, asshole. You'd better be half-dead in a ditch."

"Why don't you call him?" Tom suggested.

So I did, nicely at first. "Phil, it's DC, you know, the mafia princess. Um, did you forget? I hope everything is OK. Call me."

At 7:00, I pictured Phil sitting in a bar, chatting up other pool owners, promising to do their pools, tired of me and my neediness. I had a glass of wine and, although I knew better, I called him again. "Phil, it's DC again, and I am really disappointed. I mean, you promised you'd get the pool ready for my daughter's birthday party. I guess I am losing my patience."

The following morning there was a voice message from a slightly perturbed pool boy. "DC, it's Phil. I'm sorry you are losing your patience, but my 80-year-old mom fell and broke her arm in two places, and her hip. I was with her at the hospital all day yesterday, and I can't use my phone at the hospital. Anyway, she's just a little more important to me than your pool. I can't promise exactly when I'll get out there this week, but I will. Call me."

I was as giddy as a schoolgirl with a crush. *There's still some hope, maybe I can push the party out a week and Phil will get the pool open by then.* I began writing the script in my head ("I'm so sorry. Where do I send the flowers?"), begging Phil's forgiveness as I pressed redial.

Meanwhile, the actual title of this story? ***Zen and the Art of Pool Boy Maintenance.***

And the Twain Shall Cleave

by Lockie Hunter

"**B**e sure to stay away from the fat, gray cat. She'll bite you as soon as look at you," I explained to my fiancé, Zachary, as his car took the large "S" turn through Sam's Gap, exposing the "Welcome to the Great State of Tennessee" sign. I smiled. I was in my home state.

"The family dog is named Heidi," I continued. "We named her that because she was so scared of the bicentennial fireworks that she hid under the bed."

"My God," he said. "That's an old dog. She has to be almost 20 years old now."

"No. It's not the same dog," I said, swaying into the next curve. "That dog died when I was still in junior high. It's one continuous dog. We name every dog Heidi."

He looked baffled. "I'm not getting it," he said.

I sighed, fearing there was a lot that he wasn't going "get" about my quirky hillbilly family.

"OK, where *were* we?" I asked.

"About to take a break. Are you sure we are on the right road? We are in the middle of absolute nowhere," he said, gesturing to the surrounding mountainside that had been carved in half to make this road.

Zachary was a northerner, born in Massachusetts and raised in Maine. Though he had been south of the Mason-Dixon line, he had never before been in the Appalachian hills.

"We just passed a man shooting fish in a stream," he said.

"Stop making fun."

"Honey…there was a man standing by the stream."

"And?"

"He had a shotgun aimed squarely at the fish."

I looked to my right to see a sweet creek flowing through some dappled trees. We were nearing Flag Pond and the mountain had flattened into a lovely meadow. "More sporting and difficult than just dynamiting the fish," I said.

"Huh?"

"So where *were* we?" I asked again, eager to tutor Zachary in the details of my family life before we arrived.

"Like I said we are *taking* a break," he said. "Honey, I know the entire lineage of your family including all dogs, stray cats, and guinea pigs that ever crossed the Montgomery family threshold. I know to eat all the food on my plate and ask for seconds and dish out compliments to your mom. I know the Tennessee state bird is the chickadee. I know that your great-grandmother dipped snuff.

"I know the crew of lovely ladies spits up men and chews them out, and the only exception is your father who has managed to survive by wits alone. The entire family is matriarchal, and I think the women only keep him around to mow the lawn and get that one particular chafing dish from the high cabinet. I think your family's lawn and garden are 'award winning' because you must have all the family men buried out there somewhere adding nitrates to the soil." He took a deep breath and continued.

"I know that when I marry you, I too, will join their ranks, dying bizarrely and tragically, prime of life, not even 40, but I love you anyway and don't care."

"OK. Just so you're clear," I said and held back a smile. "My dad is still king of the house, you know. My mom just sort of makes all of the rules."

"I think your father is like a retired CEO who is on the board of directors in name only." Zac said, fiddling with the radio to find a station.

"Look, twenty miles 'til Jonesborough!" I said, jumping up in my seat. "Roll down your window and get some of that saccharine air into your Yankee lungs. It'll do you some good."

We were in Jonesborough to plan the wedding. We were to interview florists and taste butter crème frostings. My mother picked out Bible verses and stopped short when she came to a particular passage.

"The twain shall cleave," she said. "You two are the twain, and you'll be doing all the cleaving." This made her giggle.

"They'll be no cleaving in my house until *after* the wedding," my daddy said.

That evening, my fiancé charmed my family. He was a wonderful person, and his light shined brightly. I was deeply in love with this man, and I couldn't keep my hands off of him. Twice, I was caught grabbing his butt and met with disapproving glances from my father.

At dinner the conversation flowed easily. I sat back happily back in my chair—my belly full of extra-good baked brown rice and golden potato casserole—and basked in the funny stories that my Zachary told. I was happy, but I felt a twinge of anxiety. We should have continued our talk in Sam's Gap, for I knew there was something else, some quirk or idiosyncrasy that I had yet to disclose to my fiancé. There was something minor but revelatory about my family I was forgetting to tell him. I just couldn't put my finger on it.

That revelation came when Zachary emerged from the porch, his face scrunched in a frown.

"Your dad hates me," he said, pulling me aside into the pantry.

"What?"

"I was on the porch telling him how lovely his house was, and how happy his daughter made me, and he didn't say anything at all, not even a grunt."

"Well, were you talking to him, to his face, so he could see you?" I fingered a can of pole beans.

"No." Zachary shifted his foot.

"Well, Daddy's ears don't work so well. He can't hear well if you're not facing him directly."

Zachary's eyes grew wide. "I know the name of your first goldfish, but you *forgot* to mention your father is *deaf*? Is there anything else you forgot to tell me?" he asked, his arms flailing widely, knocking over a pyramid of mac-n-cheese boxes.

"Calm down, sweetie. He's not a hundred percent deaf, really, and he refuses to get a hearing aid so we don't talk about it." I smiled at my fiancé and went in for a long kiss, but he shrugged me away. I again worried that there was indeed something else I forgot to tell Zachary, but I was too full of wine and good humor to worry about it for long. I tried again for a kiss, and this one was returned with quite a bit of fire. I couldn't wait to get him into my bed tonight.

My parent's home boasts a grand foyer, a great room they call it. There are two sets of stairs. One set leads to a solitary bedroom over the garage, and one set leads to two upper bedrooms adjacent to one another, connected by a catwalk. Most visiting paramours were relegated to the room over the garage, far from the bedroom of my parent's supposed virginal daughter. It should be noted that that this particular virgin was in her early thirties and had been married once before, but on this rule they were firm.

In Boston, Zachary and I lived together in a 500-square-foot brownstone studio in the Back Bay. My parents knew we lived together. They must have reasoned that it was practical for an engaged couple, saving on rent and thus being able to have a little nest egg. I assume they imagined that he slept on the couch, and I in the bed, our fingertips gently touching at night.

Later, after the wedding, my parents would insist we stay in bed all day. They would make off-color jokes about sleeping late, so desperate were they for grandchildren, but for now, under their roof, we were to behave as if we were living in Victorian times.

So it came as a complete surprise when my father deposited Zachary's luggage in the room adjacent to mine, just a catwalk away. "They must really like you a lot!" I beamed, watching him unpack. At bedtime, he thanked my parents for the meal, kissed me goodnight, and went to his bedroom, while I retired to mine.

I dressed in something provocative and waited for my door to slide open.

He arrived ten minutes later, scented with fresh aftershave. "Hey, sexy lady," he said, as he glided into bed next to me. Shortly thereafter, a need arose. "Did you bring protection?' I asked. I was not on birth control pills, as we wanted to begin a family straight away, but, with the wedding still four months away, I had no desire to be a pregnant bride.

"It's in the other room," he said. "I'll be right back."

He didn't even grab a robe.

I waited anxiously for the return of my lover. Five minutes passed, then ten.

Finally, I grabbed my dressing gown, cinched it around my waist and walked the long hallway to his bedroom.

I found him shivering under the covers, his face watery, his brow soggy.

"What the heck happened?" I asked.

"Leave please, before he hears you," he said, pushing me away with one shaky hand.

"Who?"

"Your father..."

"What!"

Now he bolted up in bed, ready to tell a tale of terror. "I was walking to the room and I heard something from below. I looked down to see if it was the fat cat or perhaps Heidi, but I couldn't see anything, as they keep such a spotlight on this catwalk. I was completely illuminated, but downstairs was blackness." He stopped, took a deep breath, and pulled the covers tighter to him. "Then I heard it. A cough in the great room below. Yes, it was most definitely a cough, and then some mumbling with your daddy's timbre."

The revelation that I had forgotten to tell Zachary. Oh no. Not this!

"Dad doesn't really sleep. He strolls the house at night, replaying conversations with the board of directors. It's an old habit." For Zachary had been correct; my father *was* a retired CEO. And five years later, he still worried. He was an insomniac, a night owl.

"So," I asked hesitantly, "when you heard my father speak, what did you do?"

"I froze!" Zachary said, imitating his position.

"Well, you must have made quite the striking silhouette," I giggled, remembering the state of arousal he was in when he left my room.

The next morning at the breakfast table we waited for the bomb to drop. Mom was hustling around the kitchen as usual, refilling glasses of orange juice and passing out more cheesy breakfast casserole. Dad was smiling into his coffee cup while reading the morning paper. It was easy to believe that we imagined the incidents of the night before. The day progressed pleasantly.

"I don't think he knows anything," I said to Zachary, as we returned from the tuxedo shop. We were met by my mother at the front door.

"Get washed up for dinner," she said. "We are going out to the club tonight. Got to show off my future son-in-law."

I looked to Dad for confirmation.

"Honey, if she wants to go to the club, it's up to her. You know your mother gets whatever she pleases."

"OK. Let me just put on a dress shirt and tie," said Zachary, and he headed up the flight of steps to our catwalk.

"You won't find your clothes up there," said my father. His tone was pleasant, a little teasing.

"Oh?" I asked.

"Zachary here has a new bedroom for the duration of his stay. He will find his things above the garage."

"Why on God's green earth did you move him?" asked my mother.

"I just think the boy will be more comfortable up there," said my father. He winked at me, and that was the end of my romantic weekend. The rest of the week continued apace, with more meals and more laughter and each night ending with Zachary sheepishly retiring to his lonely garage bedroom.

The incident so rattled my love that, back in our brownstone in Boston, for almost a week, he removed himself to the couch, and I lay in our bed…only our fingertips touching.

Lockie Hunter *is from a town in Appalachia where oral storytelling is vital to the community. She's been known to spin quite a few tall tales, so she thought she'd make it official and get a degree in fiction (a license to lie). Thus, Lockie holds an MFA in fiction from Emerson College in Boston and teaches creative writing at Warren Wilson College. She tries to instill an appreciation for the absurd into her students, as they are the leaders of tomorrow and will need as much of a sense of humor as possible. Lockie's words have somehow found their way into numerous journals including the* Baltimore Review, Brevity, *the* Main Street Rag, The Christian Science Monitor, *and others. Her humor has appeared in* McSweeney's Internet Tendency, Opium, The Morning News, *and many other venues. Lockie is fueled by fast food, iced tea, and cheap red wine. She is writing a fat Low Country novel that it is certain to find her disinherited. You may find more of her work at* www.lockiehunter.com *and read of her teaching adventures at her new blog,* www.WritingAdjunct.wordpress.com.

Diana

by W. Bruce Cameron

Perhaps the first woman to whom I ever felt physically attracted was a beauty named Diana Dietrich. She had long, golden hair and slender legs, which she crossed and recrossed all day in a seductive manner, driving me into a state of fevered yearning.

Sometimes she would turn and smile at me and my heart would send tremors throughout my entire body—the uncertain grin I forced onto my twitching lips in return probably led her to conclude I was suffering from intestinal bloat.

I sat and schemed ways to win Diana's love, carefully constructing fantasies in which I heroically rescued her from man-eating alligators, marauding pirates, and other dangers common to the Kansas City area.

We were in third grade.

Diana was the oldest child of the school principal, so my hidden affections made me feel like I was coveting the camp commandant's daughter. Mr. Dietrich was a stern man who prowled the lunchroom and told kids they should eat their vegetables, which was how we knew he was evil. He would wander up from behind an unsuspecting student and spear him with a malevolent glare. "Aren't you going to finish your lima beans?" he'd demand in a silky whisper, standing still as an ice statue while the poor kid spooned mouthful after mouthful of the loathsome things past a shocked and disbelieving gag reflex.

In one of my fantasies, I rescued Diana from some vicious koala bears on the school bus, and from that point forward her grateful father would stop by my table, spy my untouched Brussels sprouts, and give me an avuncular wink while the other third graders gasped in amazement and voted me class president.

Toward the end of the school year, my passion still unrevealed, I began to despair of ever making Diana my girlfriend. To my bitter disappointment, no giant bats had terrorized the children on the playground, nor had floodwaters roared down the hallways, sweeping Diana within range of my manly grasp. I was going to finish out the semester with my first love totally unrequited.

Then fate intervened: I was put next to Diana in music class. Music was taught by a demented woman who truly believed we would waste our TV-viewing time practicing the flutophones we'd been issued. She would stand in front of us and wave her arms in a spastic fashion, forcefully conducting an orchestra capable of emitting only a desultory chorus of thin whistles and peeps.

Sitting next to Diana in that class, randomly tooting out flutophone notes and nodding patronizingly to the music teacher, I was seized with an impulse of masculine boldness. Moving my foot across the floor, I innocuously touched my shoe against Diana's...and left it there.

This sort of rankly overt sexual contact was unheard of in third grade; I half expected Diana to drop her plastic instrument and scream. Instead, though, Diana responded by leaving her foot in place.

I didn't dare look. Taking a shaky breath, I recklessly pushed a little harder, letting her know that this was no accident, that I really meant what I was saying with the toe of my sneaker.

And still she didn't move. If anything, she pressed back, and I nearly swooned with passion—all this time, she had been feeling the same way! I closed my eyes and let my soul guide my music, hooting like a love-sick duck.

I stroked her with my foot the entire class, and never once did she move away. At the end of the hour, when the defeated music teacher exhaustedly motioned for us to quit honking our flutophones, I turned and gave Diana a radiant, when-do-you-want-to-announce-our-engagement kind of smile.

Her response was to blink and regard me as if she had no idea why I was acting so knowing, which startled me. Weren't our feet even now locked in intimate embrace? I glanced down to assure myself that her message of affection was not being misunderstood.

My foot was pressed against the *leg of her chair*. I'd spent the whole class declaring my love to a stick of furniture!

And to this day, the haunting notes of a flutophone can instantly take me back to that heartbreaking day in third grade.

QUICKIE from DC:

If it weren't for crushes and imaginary boyfriends in grade school and high school, I may have very well ended up in the convent. (And yes, I know I would have gotten kicked out for smoking, drinking, and pulling dirty pranks, but that's not my point.) Other than a box of Valentine candy from Tommy Haupreicht in fifth grade, I was ignored: a boy-crazed wallflower—albeit a wild one—not destined to be plucked until well into my college years. My romantic adolescent memories are more in the Catholic-school-girl/ stalker-in-training category—like roller-skating past Mike Newmann's house (for hours), or waiting for Bo Seiple to come out of art class just to get a glimpse (every day for two years)—which would then make me swoon and give me those tingly feelings in places only the banana seat on my bike knew about, feelings that told me I really didn't want to be a nun after all. Thank God.

W. Bruce Cameron *is a Benchley Award winner for humor and was the 2012 NSNC Newspaper Columnist of the Year. He has written* *for TV (*8 Simple Rules, *based on his book* 8 Simple Rules for Dating My Teenage Daughter) *and cowrote the feature film* 40 is the New Dead, *which will be released in 2013.*

His novel A Dog's Purpose *spent forty-nine weeks on the* New York Times *best seller list. DreamWorks is developing it as a film and Cameron and his writing partner, Cathryn Michon, wrote the screenplay. The sequel,* A Dog's Journey, *was published in May 2012, and was instantly a* New York Times *best seller.*

Cameron's novel The Dogs of Christmas *will be published in the fall of 2013. He is currently unsure if he can even write a book without dogs in the title.*

Incident of the Drunken Wench in the Night

by Sherry Stanfa-Stanley

"When you write the story," she begged, "do you promise to be discreet?"

I agreed, knowing that "discreet" is a vague term and that verbal contracts mean shit. But I am feeling benevolent tonight, so I will acquiesce and withhold her real name. Henceforth, I shall simply refer to her as the Drunken Wench.

A nor'easter on the shores of Lake Erie, with a threatened dump of snow, is nothing to sneeze at. But we were four strong women, willing to sacrifice our well-being to attend a fund-raiser an hour away to help with a friend's medical expenses. Surely the God of Insufferable Winter Weather would acknowledge this goodness in our hearts. Besides, the evening promised great food and liquor, and that is always OK by us. We're charitable that way.

Much merriment followed: lobster and laughter and witty conversation. Meanwhile, as promised, all hell was breaking loose outside. And then I realized we had a Drunken Wench on our hands.

Her condition wasn't anticipated, considering she'd consumed a full dinner and only three glasses of wine over several hours. But sometimes the God of Liquor just looks down and laughs and claims you as his own. After witnessing her gleeful babbling to less-than-gleeful strangers, along with her Jell-O moves on the dance floor, I deduced that it was time we left.

I was the designated driver. I pushed my way through the knee-deep snowdrifts, cleaned off the SUV, and pulled up to the bar's entrance.

My sister, Lori, and a third comrade, Lisa, climbed aboard. I peered into the rearview mirror, eying the sole empty seat. The Drunken Wench was not following protocol.

"Get in," I yelled through the open car door.

My directive was met with only a curbside giggle.

"What's the problem?"

"I can't get in. My legs are a little…rubbery." More giggles.

Lisa climbed out to help. Over the howl of the nor'easter, we soon heard sounds of a more relentless force of nature. Let this be a lesson to you students of physics: Nothing is as unbudgable as a Drunken Wench with Rubbery Legs.

Lori sighed and joined them outside. I hunkered down in the driver's seat. I was already serving as designated driver. How selfless must I be?

Oh, the coaxing and pleas that ensued. "Grab my hand," "Just one more step," and "No, don't sit down in the snow, you might suffocate."

I knew futility when faced with it. I honked the horn. "Leave her here," I shouted. "We'll come back and get her tomorrow." My sympathetic nature was frostbitten. Did I mention it was cold?

Ten more minutes passed. In late-night winter-storm time, this equates to roughly six hours. My frozen hands managed to pry open my door. I took several giant steps through the snow. "Move aside," I growled at Lori.

Lori was happy to oblige; she had already laughed so hard she'd peed her pants, which had immediately frozen to her legs. She'd be forced to peel them off later.

I stood on one side of the car and pushed. Lisa stood on the other side and pulled. We pushed. We pulled. The mass that was the Drunken Wench didn't appear to understand the laws of physics. Still, we finally managed to get her half-sprawled across the backseat.

"OK, stop, stop, I'm good now. Let go," she slurred.

We hesitated before pulling our hands away. She slid off the seat into the snow.

Yet we persevered. We heaved and we hoed again, and we managed to get her entire torso back on the seat. Only her legs remained sticking out of the car. Lisa shrieked as I started to shut the door on the protruding legs, simply cramming the Drunken Wench inside like one might sit on an overstuffed suitcase. So I took, instead, to bending the legs, this way and that way, until they fit. I squinted as I peered down. That one didn't seem to be bent in an entirely natural position.

Regardless, she was in!

I slammed the door, the howl of the wind masking the whimpering that now emitted from the backseat.

Sure, she'd be bruised the next day, the Drunken Wench. But she'd wake up in the comfort of a warm bed, not a blanket of snow in front of a downtown bar. Dislocated limbs aside, I figured she'd thank us for that.

And you can bet I'll think twice before I ever again go out drinking with my mother.

QUICKIE from DC:

This was written by my younger sister. Most people who know us would likely guess the Drunken Wench to be me. In fact, when I first read it I wondered if it was me...

Sherry Stanfa-Stanley *is fond of saying she is a recent empty-nester who now devotes her spare time to caring for rescued animals. In reality, the grown children keep coming home and she caters to a bunch of spoiled and badly behaved pets. By day, Sherry is a communication director at a midwestern university, and by night she writes women's fiction, humor, and human interest stories. She has three years of archives at* <u>sherrystanfa-stanley.com</u> *and a new blog* *in the works. Sherry's work has appeared here and there, and now here... She received one of nine national fellowships in 2011 by the Midwest Writers Workshop. Her first collection of essays will be published in 2013. As of the publication date of this anthology, her mother was still speaking to her.*

Little Debbie

By Patch Rose

T his originally appeared as "Little Betty" in Patch's column and his collection, One Year To Live? A Nobody's Guide to Surviving Cancer.

Those who live in small towns know—it can take an hour to shop for cat food. That's because of all the chatty friends and neighbors you meet by the turnip greens. And when you write for the local paper, watch out, boy. Those turnip greens will leave the store before you do.

So, after ending my tenth neighborly chat, still cat food-less, I turned quickly down the wrong aisle.

And there she was.

Little Debbie.

"Wassup, baby cakes," she cooed from a box of Frosty Fudgy Squares. "Haven't seen you in a long time."

I took a deep breath and wheeled my cart right past her.

"Where you goin'?" Little Debbie breathed, this time from a box of Sugar Snap Snacks.

"Far away from you," I said, pushing the cart faster. "Now leave me be."

"Come on, cupcake," she called out from a box of cinnamon swirls. "Come and see me. We can work it out. Ain't Little Debbie been good to you?"

Oh, had Little Debbie been good to me. My whole life, I never smoked. I never drank. I didn't freebase Vicks cough syrup. But my, oh my, did I have a gripping vice. I loved to do Little Debbie.

I'd eat anything with Little Debbie's scrubbed pink midwestern face on it. Cherry Flips, Ladyfingers, Fig Bars. I dunked Debbie's donuts, nibbled her nutty bars, and greedily licked the cream from her oatmeal cream pies. Little Debbie was my wanton slut, my freak, and believe you me, I was hooked.

Bad.

Then I got brain cancer.

"Look," I told the freckled, grinning girl on the boxes of Astral Kisses. "You've been very good to me. Very good at being very bad."

She gave out a throaty laugh. I pushed my cart further. "Later, Little Debbie," I called out.

Brain tumors, you see, love sugar. My Thai Yoda neurologist made it clear at our first consultation: If I wanted to survive past six months, I had to say <u>bye-bye</u> to sugar.

I fought daily cravings for Debbie's Marshmallow Treats and Strawberry Shortcake. The withdrawal was killing me, but I was resolute. If I wanted to live, my torrid love affair with this sweet, hot eight-year-old girl had to end.

"Honey, honey," Little Debbie soothed from a box of Nut Crunch, "I've changed, baby. See? Zero grams trans fat! One-third less sodium! I got it all going on, all for you, sweet thing!"

I stopped short, stared hard into her cornflower blue eyes. "And how much sugar you got, sugar?"

From a box of Devil Bites, I thought I saw a blush darken those freckled cheeks. "Ah, come on, mini muffin…"

I snatched up her Sweet Rolls. (Oh, God…Little Debbie's Sweet Rolls!) I flipped Debbie over and scanned her backside.

Thirty-two grams of sugar.

"Pure poison," I told her. "I'm out." I started to replace the box.

"Baby," she whispered. "Don't I feel good in your arms?"

Oh, did Little Debbie feel good in my arms. I brought the box up to my nose, inhaling her sweet perfume: granulated sugar cane smothered in fructosey fudge. It was like slipping into a chocolate Jacuzzi.

My resolve melted like a Hershey's kiss. I looked over each shoulder, then I slipped Debbie into my cart.

She purred at me. "You won't regret it, honey buns."

I felt high, jazzed. I jumped onto the back of the cart and popped a wheelie. Debbie laughed. I laughed too, nervously flushed with nectary delight.

And there he was. He was seventeen or so, a pretty young thing. He bopped down the aisle, his jeans held on by nothing but hipbone. His silky long hair bounced as he jived. He wore sneakers and a T-shirt that said, "Eat Peaches."

Peach Boy gave me a "s'up?" head nod. Then, he looked down at my Little Debbie.

"Hi sugar," she cooed up at him. "Wanna try something sweet?"

"Little Hussy!" I hissed. I flung the box to the floor. "Skanky Ho-Ho!" I stomped away in disgust, leaving Debbie and my empty cart in the middle of the snack aisle.

"You'll be back!" she shrieked. "They always come back! Ain't nobody can quit Little Debbie!"

I fled around the corner into the beans and pet food aisle, my hands clammy and shaking. Behind me, I heard Little Debbie's silky voice rising from the floor. She was working Peach Boy, hard.

"Forget him, sugar cube. You wanna try my Jelly Roll?"

I snatched four cans of cat food from the shelf and bolted for the front of the store.

And there she was. Sylvia, my wife, stood waiting at the checkout. I guess she'd come in to buy some things on her way home.

I looked at her purchases. Wheat pasta. Green tea. And no-sugar peanut butter.

When I got cancer, my wife started making food she didn't like, because it was what I needed to live. In the process, she left behind her own Little Debbie. White bread. White rice. Potatoes. She gave them all up, to save me.

Sylvia turned and saw me. Her eyes grew bigger than root beer barrels. Her face lit up like a lemon drop. She waved to me, her smile warm, sweet and smooth as Caramello.

I knew right then that Little Debbie was wrong. I *could* quit her. I could spend the rest of my days quitting her. My life was sweet enough.

As I joined Sylvia at the checkout, and checked out her creamy white, Haagen-Dazs face, I suddenly remembered my wife's life-long nickname: Cookie.

QUICKIE from Susan:

Patch Rose was a wonderful man who was worried like hell he'd be sued for this piece. Unfortunately, Patch lost his battle with cancer in February 2009. His wife, Cookie, said we were right in recognizing Little Debbie—that little tart—right away. As a semi-rednecky Georgia girl, I still love Little Debbies even though they gave me a front fanny and encouraged the vast and fast production of cellulite all over some key body parts. Now, am I scared of being sued? Not on your life. Will I eat more Little Debbies? You bet your sweet rippled ass.

In November 2005, Herald reporter and freelance writer **Patch Rose** was diagnosed with a GBM brain tumor. Statistically, GBM patients live about one year after diagnosis. His book, One Year To Live? is based on Patch Rose's true-life story. "What's the most basic, fundamental lesson I have learned from my cancer experience? Don't open suppository wrappers with your teeth," is a typical quip--mining humor while tip-toeing around land-mines—from the book.

That same year Patch won the coveted Mona Schreiber Prize for X Marks The Spot, "A wonderfully absurd rumination on the religious practice of Ash Wednesday," according to Brad Schreiber—founder of the contest. Brad wrote a story about Patch and the meaning of "writers community" after learning of his death in 2009. "He was a man who managed to make a scar on the side of his head look as natural as his smile. He was one of the most vibrant people I have ever met."

Patch's series of columns compiled in book form won first place in its category in the New Mexico Press in 2007 and was chosen as the editors' favorite in Fifty Shades of Funny: Hook-ups, Break-ups, and Crack-ups. Three years after Patch's passing, he remains an important part of our writers' community. To view the full article, go to http://redroom.com/member/brad-Schreiber/writing/patch-rose-and-the-meaning-of-a-writers-community

The Little Black Dress

By Lisa Brower

Back when my husband and I were still dating, I made the mistake of asking him the most loaded question any woman can ask a man. No, not "Do you love me?" but "What is your fantasy?" Remember, we were still dating, so there was a possibility that I might fulfill it depending on how depraved it was. He gave me a surprising answer—he fantasized about being seduced by a woman in a rubber dress and boots. OK, maybe I'm just easily surprised, but in any event, I thought, "Oh hell, I can do this; it's not too weird."

Well, he deployed with his unit the next week, leaving me to plan for this event for the next six months. As small as our town is, we do have a lingerie shop that stocks such items; it's hidden on a small street in Remerton and only patronized after dark by local residents. I parked my car at a restaurant nearby and walked through the back way to get there like every other local does. Sure enough, she did stock an entire wardrobe of rubber clothing; obviously my new love was not the only freak in town. For $49.95 plus tax, I purchased a pantyhose-sized package with a shiny-rubber-clad seductress pictured on the front, plus it came with a roll-on of "rubber shine" to give it that "wet" look. The salesgirl told me to roll it on after I got the dress on. She stressed that part, and later this would come in handy. I drove home and threw the package in a drawer and waited for my sweetheart to get home.

In June, he arrived home safely. I gave him a few weeks to rest up before I sprung my surprise on him, because I am thoughtful that way. Finally the designated night arrived. My son, the Jimster, was at his dad's for the weekend. My stomach looked flatter than usual. It was time to roll that dress out.

I slipped into the bathroom while he was involved with the History Channel, dress and boots tucked under my arm. When I opened the package, the strong smell of rubber wafted out; actually, it smelled like a new shower curtain, so I opened the window. The dress came with instructions, which was a bit intimidating. "Make sure exposed skin is dry. Remove all lotions and apply talcum powder to all areas." I got a towel and buffed off all the glitter lotion I had just liberally applied. I patted powder lightly onto my skin and stretched the dress over my head. It was about the size of a bicycle inner tube in diameter.

Damn, why didn't I look at it before? I got it over my head without pulling out too much hair—it felt like a giant rubber scrunchie—but I got stuck mid-chest. I managed to get an arm down and reached for the baby powder to ease the transition. The dress had rolled up like a vacuum cleaner belt around my chest and was squeezing off my oxygen. I managed to escape and decided to bring it up from the bottom instead. I stepped in and started easing it up a centimeter at a time, pausing to powder myself liberally every two inches or so. I was starting to resemble a breaded cutlet, and the powerful rubbery stench of the dress was making me dizzy. I got it up enough to where I could stretch the halter strap around my neck and turned to the mirror to view the dangerous seductress I was sure I would see.

I did not look one thing like the girl in the picture on the package. She had curves; I was completely flattened into a dusty black rubber tube. Turning to the side was not much better; my boobs were not flattered by being squashed downward by rubber. I fluffed, puffed, rearranged, and still things were not looking good. Plus there was powder all over this horror. Time for the "rubber shine"; maybe that was what was missing. I screwed off the top and started to roll the shine over the dress. It smelled like Armor-All, was greasy, and turned the powder to grayish sludge. This was not going anywhere like how I expected, but there was no turning back now. I was now sweating from the exertion of wrestling on the dress, and covered with baby powder and lemon-scented silicone.

I fixed myself up as well as possible, slipped on the high-heeled boots, and exited the bathroom to get my man. What I then learned was that any step caused the dress to snap up like a broken window shade, landing around my waist and compressing any stomach and rear fat into a bulging horror. Pulling the hem down, I began to glide toward the living room like a foot-bound geisha. I made it to the bedroom door and knew I didn't dare to try to get any farther.

I posed in the frame of the doorway and whistled to get Chuck's attention. He'd better have still been awake after all I had just gone through. He turned around in his armchair, coffee cup in hand, and gasped with what I hoped was lust. He got up and started heading toward the bedroom, and I glided as quickly as possible to the bed before the dress attacked again. I arranged myself on the bed holding on to the hem with my greasy hand, trying to take a deep breath. He flopped down next to me and ran his hand down the front of the dress.

"What is this stuff?" he asked as he wiped his hand off on his jeans. "What's that smell?"

"Never mind that," I purred. "How does it look?"

He answered by trying to pull me closer without actually touching the dress again. It was then that the heat of the moment was shattered by the embarrassing sound of a huge fart. It was the dress. It had formed an air bubble between my ribcage and navel that expelled an explosion of sound every time I moved. I rolled back on to my back and pressed the bubble again. "FFFLLLAARRPP," went the dress. I began to laugh hysterically. I had spent over fifty dollars and an hour in the bathroom to purchase a very unsexy whoopee cushion. I amused myself for several minutes making the dress expel air and laughed so hard I began to snort. My future husband looked disappointed, as the moment for him was most definitely gone for the evening. "Why do you smell like a tire?" he asked.

"Never mind," I answered. "Let me get this thing off. I've got to have a shower."

"Need help?" he offered hopefully, still trying to salvage the mood.

I struggled out of the dress as much as I struggled to get in it. You will sweat in a rubber dress on a hot, south Georgia night, no matter how low you set your air conditioner.

We never discussed the abysmal end of my poor husband's fantasy again: I had killed it dead in that awful dress, which I'm sure I probably could have found a use for, maybe to patch tires or the hose. It turned out later that he had never seen a dress like that on a real woman, only in a magazine, which explained quite a bit. I thought about explaining the art of airbrushing, and that they probably cut the dress up the back to mold it to the model in the photo, but that was just stabbing the already-dead horse. I know when to let an issue go when it's necessary, and this was one of those times. Sometimes silence is good in a marriage, and things left unspoken should remain so.

Lisa Brower wound her way through a dizzying path of careers; from punked out fashionista hair dresser/ underdressed strip club cocktail waitress, crusading social worker/ poor single mother, to prim librarian/ dedicated military wife, and finally to blissed out massage therapist/ tortured comedy writer. She has been a contributor to the Huffington Post and NPR. She is currently living in Nashville, Georgia. Her website is www.prettybutshallow.com.

Oh, Those Sexual Side Effects

by Leslie Marinelli

A few years back, several months after my second child was born, I was suffering from a pretty soul-crushing case of postpartum depression.

After bursting into a rash of maniacal tears and confessing "very dark thoughts" at my annual checkup in response to the clearly antagonistic query of "What's new?", I was promptly escorted 'round the corner to a psychiatrist for some happy pills.

I wrote the following story two weeks later:

So there is good news and bad news. The good news is that the cocktail of antidepressants I've been on for two weeks seems to be working! I'm not nearly as negative and overwhelmed as I was a few weeks ago. Hallelujah! The bad news is the absolute *cavalcade* of side effects. Apparently that is the big trade off with most SSRIs: feel better mentally/feel worse physically.

Well I found out the hard way what all those antidepressant commercials mean by "sexual side effects." I had always wondered, "What *is* that? When they say 'low risk of sexual side effects,' does that mean you're less likely to start humping inanimate objects, grow hair on your palms, or suddenly have a penchant for farm animals?" No, it's nothing like that. "Sexual side effects" specifically means loss of libido (so what's new?), inability to achieve an erection (men) or attain sufficient lubrication (ladies), and/or an inability to achieve orgasm.

Insert sound of screeching tires and crashing car.

Hold it right there, Dr. Feelgood. *Excuse me?* Did you say "inability to achieve an orgasm"?

Look, if I am going to clean up my nether-regions, get all sweaty, and soil my sheets, there needs to be some kind of a prize at the end of *that* carnival game. In other words, "I gots to get mine's, m'kay?"

I'm obviously no expert, but I'm willing to wager that orgasms would probably be beneficial to treating clinical depression. And the more the merrier, right? So why on God's green Earth would I want to take away one of the few remaining rays of sunshine in my life? Talk about depressing. Sheesh. This alone may be worth going off the meds. But wait, there's more.

In addition to not being able to reach the top of Tingle Mountain, my new antidepressants have rendered me incredibly constipated. This is a problem, friends. I'm a big fan of pooping. I make Jamie Lee Curtis look repressed and anal-retentive. Not being able to drop the kids at the pool each morning could be a real deal breaker.

Honestly, even with the new influx of serotonin coursing through my brain, without my daily downstream release of the Chattahoochee Brown Trout, I'm feeling meaner than a sack full of rattlesnakes. And keeping all that unpleasantness bottled up inside for so long leads to the next unpleasant side effect: *flatulence.*

Remember the campfire scene in *Blazing Saddles*? Worse. Way worse. You know your beef darts are lethal when even the dog leaves the room. I've seen him nosh in the litter box, for crying out loud, so if even the dog won't give me a proper canine greeting, you know it's bad.

Truly, this gas is like *nothing* I have ever smelled before, which is how I know it must be a product of the strange chemicals I'm ingesting every day. I'm talking paint-peelers, folks. Even my feisty daughter, who *loves* a good "pull my finger" joke, won't play along. She's all, "Whoa, Mama...was that YOU? I thought maybe the doggie ate another frog. Remember that?" Nice.

Which brings us right back to the main issue of sexual side effects: y'all, there is nothing that will ruin the mood or spoil your ability to achieve a good old fashioned toe-curler like an unintentional Dutch oven. (Sorry about that last one, honey...I'll try to give you a heads-up next time.)

Oh, but we're just getting warmed up, folks! (Bah-dump-bump-tchhhh.) There is also dry mouth, dizziness, rashes, weight gain, and headaches. Is this an antidepressant or birth control? I mean, damn! Because seriously, there is definitely *no* baby-makin' goin' on in my house right now. Maybe I'll put the kids on SSRIs when they get to high school to keep them from getting knocked up.

So, only time will tell: Will the improved mental health be enough to compensate for all these crazy side effects? Or will my new sense of optimism be blown asunder by all the sexual frustration (and wafting)? You have questions. I'll have answers. Tune in next time for another riveting episode of *The Bearded Iris: Battling Depression from the Bottom Up.*

Epilogue (six years later):

Wow. Looking back on that time in my life I am immediately struck with how difficult it was to weigh the numerous pros and cons of being on antidepressants. I remember so clearly how pessimistic I felt before my brain chemistry got the little kick-start it so desperately needed. I was actually at the end of my rope and I'm surprised I was able to harness so much humor to cope when I really felt so sad and lost inside.

Gosh, if only I had sought Tom Cruise's advice instead of my own team of highly trained professionals, I would have known that vitamins and exercise were all I really needed and to stop "masking my symptoms" and start feeling better.

Bitch, please. Tom may clearly be an expert on women and mental health (jump on couches much?), but those drugs saved my life.

So here's how it all panned out:

I continued to see my psychiatrist about every six weeks to tweak my dosage and try different meds until we found a combo that would give me the best possible mental health with the least amount of physical side effects. I'm not going to lie; it took about eight months to uncover that magic combination. But once we did, my life changed dramatically for the better.

The gas disappeared. The libido perked up. My skin and weight evened out. The sound of my kids crying didn't make me feel like veering into oncoming traffic. I was able to resume a normal healthy sex life.

And I was happy.

So happy, in fact, that one day I noticed my period was late. And my breasts were sore. And no...could it be? Was I?

Yep. Pregnant. It was one of those full-circle moments Elton John's always singing about. And yet there I was, glowing and happy and bursting with good news. I went off the meds right away, had a healthy pregnancy, and eleventy months later, I was icing my hoo-hoo and holding a beautiful new baby boy.

We named him *Wellbutrin Effexor*, but we call him Bucket Head for short.

QUICKIE from Susan:

I once poisoned my husband for days with Prozac, after I'd told my doctor he needed medicated.

For one, he was way too horny. (My husband, not the doctor, at least not that I know of.)

Second, he was the grouchiest anus on the planet. (Again, my husband, not the doctor.) In fact, he was so nice he wrote a double 'script.

The result: Unfortunately, the pills I crushed in his tea bubbled up in little white lumps and boom! I was busted.

It's my belief that if we marry assholes, we have the right to legally pump them up with Prozac or any other antidepressant deemed necessary to keep the peace. And to keep our legs closed for at least one night.

While I'm on hubby number two, I would not rule out adding a bit of de-horning happy powders to his double protein shakes. Makes sense to me.

Leslie Marinelli *is a humorist, editor, and blogger currently living in the suburbs of Atlanta, Georgia. She created her blog,* <u>The Bearded Iris: A Recalcitrant Wife and Mother Tells All</u>*, in 2008, to relieve the tedium of being an invisible vessel for grandchildren and PTA donations. Today she is a BlogHer Voice of the Year, a* Babble.com *Top 100 Mom Blogger, and a Circle of Moms Top 25 Funny Mom. She also* <u>tweets</u> *like she parents: loudly and with a lot of apologies.*

Boys Have a Penis

by Robin O'Bryant

Boys have a penis, and girls have a coo-coo. That's what the girls at my house have anyway. I realize there has been all manner of research done about teaching your children the correct names for their, *ahem*, parts and how by saying *penis* and *vagina* to your children, they will be closer to you somehow by realizing how open and accepting you are of their sexuality. Hell, I even saw one mother on Oprah say the word 'clitoris' to her ten-year old. But Lord help me, I *cannot* say *vagina* to my daughters.

I tried, I really did. I had a professor in college who convinced me that if I would only say *vagina*, all my worries about my daughters being sexually promiscuous or having their lives turn into a Lifetime movie would magically disappear.

This seemed like a great theory until I actually had to say the word *vagina* to my daughter. I don't remember exactly how the conversation came up, but I do remember feeling like a complete and total pervert. It didn't help matters that as soon as the word was out of my mouth, she began chanting "bagina-bagina-bagina-bagina-bagina."

"Oops," I thought. "I have made a big mistake; quite possibly a huge mistake. She is going to go to preschool tomorrow and tell everyone she sees that she has a vagina."

Maybe you live in a liberal big city where the teacher would smile and nod approvingly at your openness as a mother, but I don't. I live in the Deep South where even women in their thirties with three kids pray their parents think they are still virgins. I had to fix this. Now.

I scrambled to cover my tracks. I thought of every acceptable nickname I could for the old "va-jay-jay," just to distract my daughter from her new favorite word.

"Va-jay-jay, Aubrey, you can call it a va-jay-jay. Or pee-pee!" I frantically tried to find a substitute.

"Bagina-bagina-BAGINA," she chanted.

"Or, or a cookie! You can call it a cookie!"

"NO, Momma! You not eat it!" She squealed and giggled. I was about to disagree.

"Coo-coo, Aubrey it's called your coo-coo!" And thus the *coo-coo* was born at our house.

The penis conversation came along only a few weeks later, when Aubrey saw her daddy peeing in the bathroom.

"You an ele-pant, Daddy?" she asked. "Momma, that Daddy's coo-coo?" I cringed all the way down to my Southern Baptist roots as I said, "No, baby. (Sigh.) That is his penis."

"Oh, he have a long coo-coo, Momma?"

"Yes, baby," I answered, already wanting to change the subject. It wasn't necessary. She wasn't very excited about the word *penis*. Smart girl...or so it seemed for a couple of years.

By the time Aubrey was four, she had a newfound interest in all things genitalia. Every bath time was peppered with questions about her own body and anyone else's she could think to ask about. I used the opportunity to remind her that her body was *hers*. It was private and she shouldn't show it to anyone else, and if anyone tried to look at her coo-coo or touch it she should always tell me.

To hopefully decrease their ever-growing interest, my husband tried to avoid being naked in front of the girls. Even so, we occasionally found ourselves discussing penises with our preschool daughters.

On Aubrey's last day of preschool, we were all dressed and ready for school so I let the girls watch SpongeBob (whom I detest) until time to leave for school. As I was checking my e-mail I overheard Aubrey say, "I hope *he* doesn't have a penis."

Brakes squealed in my head. Lord, *have* mercy.

"Aubrey, come here!"

Aubrey walked towards me with a little sideways grin, "What?"

"Um, what did you just say?" (We were about to leave for her last day of preschool and I didn't want to remember this day as "the day Aubrey told her classmates about SpongeBob's penis.")

Aubrey began giggling uncontrollably, "Hee-hee, penis."

"Do you know what that is?"

She actually snorted she was laughing so hard, "Yep, it's a boy's coo-coo."

Sigh.

"That's right, but it's private (Hello World!) and we don't talk about it at school."

Aubrey was still snickering as she walked back to the living room, "OK, Momma."

We made it through the last day of school and I thought we were safe for a while. I mean I have three girls. Surely, we could let the penis conversation rest for a bit.

A few weeks later, one of my best friends needed someone to watch her four-year old son while she and her hubby sneaked off for their anniversary. I was glad to help, because Sara is one of my favorite people in the universe. The girl has more energy than anyone I've ever met and every time she comes to my house, it's always clean when she leaves, and all my kids have been bathed. I don't actually understand how she does it, but I love her so much that I'd do just about anything for her.

Her son, Tristan, is every bit as sweet as his momma and both Aubrey and Emma claim him as their best friend. His parents are raising him to be a true gentleman by making him open doors for my little girls and assist them in pulling their bicycles out of ditches and making him stay out of their way when they are changing clothes or using the restroom. The kids are really quite funny about it, slamming doors in each other's faces and saying, "Excuse me, I *meed* some pwivacy!"

But because Aubrey had been so inquisitive about all things genitalia lately, my Mommy Radar was on high alert for any hanky-panky of the preschool persuasion. It rained nonstop on one of the days Tristan spent with us, and that led to lots of fort building and movie watching.

It was late in the afternoon. Aubrey, Emma, and Tristan were lined up on a pallet on the floor, snuggled up together watching a movie. I was in the kitchen starting dinner when I heard some mischievous giggles coming from the living room. I immediately expected the worst and tried to sneak around the corner to spy on them and catch them in the act of "I'll Show You Mine-You Show Me Yours," to no avail. Every time I popped my head around a corner, Aubrey and Tristan would be staring at the TV trying to look innocent, while Emma snoozed beside them, oblivious.

We continued this cat and mouse game for about fifteen minutes, at which point Emma had fallen asleep. I picked her up and put her between Aubrey and Tristan to separate them. If I couldn't catch them in the act, this was the best I could do.

Several days after Tristan's parents returned from their trip, Aubrey walked into my bathroom while I was taking a bath, and began yet *another* drawn-out conversation on her favorite topic.

"Mommy, why your coo-coo not look like mines?"

"Because I'm a grownup, Aubrey. Kids and grownups don't look the same."

"Oh, you have a grownup coo-coo and Daddy has a grownup penis. Right Momma?"

"Yes, baby…" (Big sigh.)

"Not like Tristan, he just has a *little tiny* kid-sized penis!"

"*What?*" I screeched.

Her eyes were wide in shock, as she realized she had just busted herself and wasn't sure what to do about it.

"Aubrey, how do you know what Tristan's penis looks like? Did he show it to you?"

She bit her bottom lip and wrinkled her nose and forehead. "Wellllll, I *think* so."

"What do you mean, you *think* so? Did you show him your coo-coo?"

She nervously pulled at her curls and twisted her hands together. "Ummmm…maybe just a little bit. I did…but, Momma,

Daddy has a big long grownup penis and Tristan just has a kid-sized one like this…" She held up her left hand in front of her left eye in the universal symbol for OK and squinted through the eraser-sized hole made by her fingers. "It's just this big, Momma."

After I herniated part of my large intestine from trying so hard not to laugh in her face, I discussed once again how her body is hers, it is private, and we are not supposed to be showing it to folks — especially boys. I called Tristan's mom so she could talk to him, and prayed fervently that our obsession with all things penile was over.

At bedtime about a week later, I was lying in Aubrey and Emma's bedroom saying our prayers and making up silly stories, when Emma busted out with, "Momma, I hab one, two, free nuts!" She unfolded three fingers as she counted them out.

Aubrey began giggling uncontrollably.

Oh Sweet, Sweet Lord in Heaven…not Emma too.

"You have three *what*?" I was nervous, y'all. *Really, really* nervous.

"*Nuts*, Momma! I said…" She leaned forward to scream in my face, "*I hab free nuts!*"

Aubrey couldn't even open her eyes and lay curled on her side in the fetal position holding her stomach she was laughing so hard.

Emma jumped off the bed and went running out of the room to tell her daddy that she had "free nuts."

I was so scared to ask the most obvious question, but I'm their momma and it had to be done…"Aubrey, what is a nut?"

"Sumpin' a squirrel eats, Momma!" She squealed and continued to laugh hysterically. "Emma is *soooo* silly!"

I took a deep cleansing breath before replying, "Yes. Yes, she is."

Robin O'Bryant *is a humor columnist and stay-at-home-mother to three daughters born within four years. She finally figured out where babies come from and got herself under control. Her first book,* Ketchup is a Vegetable and Other Lies Moms Tell Themselves, *has been rated #1 by reader reviews on* Amazon *in two genres, Humor Essays and Parenting & Families, since December 2011. O'Bryant won the South Carolina Press Association's award for Best Humor Column for 2012.*

She was a Circle of Mom's Top 25 Funniest Moms 2011 and 2012. Babble *has listed* <u>Robin's Chicks</u> *as a Top 10 Funniest Parenting Blog, and her work has been featured on* Huffington Post. *She uses her blog and newspaper columns to teach women helpful tips such as: how to breastfeed behind your back,* how to talk to your daughters about man parts, and how to write a proper goldfish obituary.*

*Only applies to lactating women with a DD cup or larger.

Waiting for Dustin

by Felice Prager

Originally published in Chocolate for a Teen's Heart *(Simon &*
Schuster).

When I was fifteen years old, I saw a movie called *The
Graduate*. I saw it with my best girlfriend, Terri, and
together, we both fell in love with the star, Dustin Hoffman. We
made a best friend's vow that one of us would marry Dustin
Hoffman and live happily ever after in a large mansion with
a swimming pool, oversized closets, and maids in Southern
California, even though we knew from publicity that he was a
New Yorker. That was just a minor detail. We had read that he
was originally from California, so the details in the picture could
change again. He could move back. Why not? We were optimistic
and in love. We thought his nose was cute. And we were fifteen
and nothing else mattered.

We read that he was thirty. We didn't see this as a problem.
There were many women who married older men. The world was

open to everything when we were fifteen. Someday we would be twenty and he would be thirty-five, and that didn't sound quite so bad. And when we turned fifty, he would be sixty-five. With time, the gap would lessen.

Terri and I also swore we'd always be best friends and we wouldn't be jealous of each other. Whoever got Dustin Hoffman was fine, as long as it was one of us. We could have adult sleepover parties and then the other one would have time with Dustin Hoffman, too.

Terri and I went to see *The Graduate* whenever we could. We cut school one day and stayed at the movies until <u>five p.m.</u> watching Dustin be Benjamin Braddock. We stopped going to Hebrew school completely and went to the movies instead. We joked about how God wouldn't mind us being at the movies because he'd like Dustin as much as we did because Dustin was so cute. Terri had heard that Dustin was Jewish, which made it even better.

We went to the movies so much that we knew the dialogue by heart. "Plastics!" we both said at the appropriate time. "Are you trying to seduce me, Mrs. Robinson?" we both said on cue. We knew the soundtrack by heart and knew exactly when each Simon and Garfunkel song would be in the background.

I stayed up late one night to see Dustin interviewed by Johnny Carson. I used my parent's Polaroid to take a photo of Dustin right off the TV screen. I slept with the photo under my pillow. The photo had stripes through it, but it was a picture of Dustin.

I bought magazines and a construction worker's lunch box. I glued all of my magazine pictures of Dustin onto the lunchbox and covered it with many layers of shellac. I spilled some shellac on the new lilac carpet in my bedroom and disguised it by rearranging my furniture while my mother was away at work. I carried my Dustin box wherever I went. I thought it made a statement about who I was.

I put Dustin's picture in a locket and wore it around my neck. I wrote his name all over my notebook. I put hearts around it. I practiced saying "Felice Hoffman" until it just rolled off my tongue. "Felice and Dustin Hoffman." "Dustin and Felice Hoffman." "Mrs. Dustin Hoffman." "Felice and Dusty Hoffman."

Then I read in the *New York Times* that Dustin was going to star in an off-Broadway play called *Jimmy Shine*. When the tickets went on sale, Terri and I cut school again to buy tickets to see Dustin Hoffman live on stage. We lived in New Jersey, so we had to go into New York to get the tickets. Up to this point, our parents hadn't let us go into Manhattan alone. They were afraid we might be mugged. They were afraid we wouldn't be able to take care of ourselves. We conveniently forgot the rules. We spent as much as we had to get the best tickets we could afford. Our parents never found out that we went into New York to get the tickets. We were very sly.

On the day of the play, I borrowed my dad's expensive new binoculars. I needed them to see Dustin's face. I needed to see him smile. I needed to see him frown. I needed to see his eyes and lips. I had it bad. I didn't tell my dad I borrowed his binoculars.

Terri and I thought the play was wonderful, although neither of us paid much attention to the plot. We were looking at Dustin's expressions. We were watching him move. We were in the same room as Dustin Hoffman. We were breathing air that might have gone through his lungs. (We held our breath a lot to keep Dustin breath inside our lungs.)

We planned to try to see him as he exited the theater, so we left before the curtain calls, found the stage door, and planted ourselves right in front of it. We were the first ones there. In doing this, I left my dad's binoculars in the theater and never saw them again. Some time later, when my dad couldn't find his binoculars and asked me if I'd seen them, I acted innocent, shrugged my shoulders, and said, "You mean the new ones? Last I saw them they were in the hall closet."

A crowd formed around us. We became animals in order to keep our front spots. We were here first. We were pushing people back, using our nails. I was pushing people with my Dustin Hoffman lunchbox. We were elbowing strangers who kept pushing. The door opened, and there was a hush. One after another, theater people left, but there was no sign of Dustin Hoffman. Terri began to panic, "What if we're at the wrong door!" I began to hyperventilate, "What if he already left!"

Then the door opened, and it was Dustin. He exited and he looked even better in person. Terri whispered into my ear, "His nose doesn't look half as big in person." I pushed my playbill toward him, and he signed it, as if this happened every night. But that didn't matter.

While he was signing my playbill, my hand touched his. I had touched Dustin Hoffman; my skin had brushed his skin. I didn't wash my hand for two weeks. I wore a glove long before Michael Jackson was the Gloved One. I took the glove off and stared at my fingers. My hand looked different now that it had touched Dustin. It looked older, more sophisticated, much more sensitive.

At this time, my mother worked in an office as a secretary, and I worked part-time at this office doing filing. In the back room of the office, there were a ton of phone books. The filing cabinets were in the back room.

Instead of filing one day, I picked up the Manhattan directory. It was a few years old. For some reason, I decided to look up Dustin Hoffman.

And it was there.

Dustin Hoffman was listed in the Manhattan phone book.

I was dying.

There was his name.

There was his address.

There was his phone number.

I tore the page out of the phone book. I memorized the phone number and shoved the torn page into my pocket. I was getting dizzy, I was so excited.

If anyone in the office needed a Manhattan phone number for anyone from Hobson, D to Hoffman, R, they were out of luck.

I went to the backroom phone and dialed Dustin's number.

It rang a few times, and then someone answered the phone.

"Hello," said the voice. It was Dustin Hoffman. I couldn't breathe.

"Hello," the voice at the other end of the phone repeated.

I hung up.

I was a mess. I had heard Dustin Hoffman on the phone. I had heard his voice. I had been electrically connected to him. I had been on the phone with the movie star I would someday marry.

And then I realized I had just hung up on a movie star. I'd hung up on Dustin Hoffman.

I picked up the phone again. I had to apologize. I had to make it right.

I redialed Dustin's number.

He answered the phone. "Hello?"

I tried to hide my shaking voice to say hello this time, but when I opened my mouth, nothing came out.

"Hello!" he said again.

Now he was barking.

"Hello!" he shouted.

"Who is it?" he yelled.

Then he slammed the phone down.

I was miserable.

I'd made Dustin Hoffman angry. I'd ruined everything.

I couldn't do filing. I couldn't work. I made believe I didn't feel well and went home early.

I was on the phone all night with Terri. I repeated the details of the two phone calls. Terri was angry because I called him without her being there.

She said she didn't have a chance to hear him. She said since I broke the pact, all was fair in love and war. She said when she married Dustin Hoffman, she would never invite me to her mansion in Beverly Hills.

I tried to calm her down. I didn't want Terri angry with me. I told her I had a better idea. She loved it, I loved it, we planned it for Monday morning.

By nine a.m., we were standing in front of Dustin Hoffman's brownstone apartment. We were cutting school again, and we were in New York. And now that we were here, neither of us knew what to do next. There was a lot of giggling. There was a lot of discussion. And then there was a lot more giggling.

Finally, we got brave and walked up the stairs. We were holding hands and moving very slowly. We entered the vestibule to Dustin Hoffman's building. On one wall were a few names with buzzers next to them. And there it was: "D. Hoffman." It was as simple and as innocuous as J. Smith or L. Jones.

We stood there giggling, and then Terri got brave and pushed the button beside Dustin's name. She pushed it and then we ran, back outside and down the stairs. We were laughing and hysterical and crying, and we just ran. When we finally stopped, we looked at each other, turned, started to laugh, and, arm in arm, we marched back to Dustin's apartment.

We climbed the stairs once again, entered the vestibule, and bravely rang his buzzer. And this time we waited. And we waited. And we waited. No one was there.

We decided to get out of there. I put my hand on the label "D. Hoffman" for good luck. My nail accidentally slid under the label, and I accidentally peeled it off. I put my lips to the dirty, gummy label, and I kissed it. Then I put it in my pocket and we left.

A few weeks later, we decided to repeat our trip to visit Dustin Hoffman. We giggled like the first time. We decided that if he were home, we'd ask for his autograph as a starter. We figured he'd ask us in for a Coke or some coffee, and we'd be so charming back that he'd ask for our phone numbers so we could spend more time together. We climbed the stairs, rang the buzzer, and held our breath. There was a new label, but again, there was no answer. Terri accidentally slid her nail under the new name label and accidentally tore it off. Now we both owned a piece of Dustin Hoffman.

Time moved on, and Terri and I parted ways, and with that my infatuation with Dustin Hoffman became unimportant. For that period in my life, I thought Dustin Hoffman was the reason I had to get up each day, but with Terri gone, it was no longer important.

I think I remember hearing Dustin Hoffman in an interview mentioning that he no longer lived in New York, that for years he sublet the old apartment that we'd once visited. He said nothing about the phone calls or the address labels. He had no memory of a young girl's hand brushing his when he signed her playbill.

Today, one of my sons is two months shy of thirteen years old. A few months ago, I helped him get tickets for an upcoming Britney Spears concert by taking turns dialing until we got through to Ticketmaster. By the time we got through, the tickets were almost sold out. As I write this, the concert is nineteen days away. My son has had the days until the concert counted out on a calendar since day 188. A day hasn't gone by when he hasn't said, "Guess how many more days until I see Britney Spears."

My son's bedroom has vaulted ceilings. On every open space of wall, he has a picture of Britney Spears. The girls in school cut pictures out of magazines for him so he can decorate his room. They know he has it bad.

When Britney's newest CD was released, my son asked me to go wait on line for it so he could be the first one in his class to own it. He made me buy two copies of it with his allowance, one for his room and one to play in the car. At the end of the school year, he threw out his loose-leaf notebook: On the cover, I saw the words, "Britney and Steven Prager."

This morning, my son said he might send Britney a letter asking if he can meet her after the concert. "I have nothing to lose," he said. "Maybe she'll read it and call me and I'll get a chance to meet her in person. It could happen."

"Maybe she will," I replied, thinking how close the apple has fallen to the tree and wondering if Dustin Hoffman would be taking his kid to the concert, too.

Felice Prager is a freelance author and multisensory educational therapist from Scottsdale, Arizona. She is the author of five books: Waiting in the Wrong Line, Negotiable and Non-Negotiable Negotiations, TurboCharge Your Brain, SuperTurboCharge Your Brain, *and* Quiz It: ARIZONA. *Prager's sixth book,* How to be the Coolest Parent on the Block, *is slated for publication in the fall of 2012. Her essays have been published locally, nationally, and internationally in print and on the Internet. You can find out more about Felice Prager's books and view samples of her writing at* http://www. FelicePrager.com .

Dispatches from the Unemployment Line

by Lisa Golden

My husband had finished doing our taxes and we were sitting down to go over them. It might have been the single most organized thing we did in our lives.

"So our income dropped by about two-thirds between 2009 and 2010." He confirmed what we had already suspected: We'd felt the pinch since I'd been laid off in late 2009 and collecting unemployment benefits while I looked for a new position, but now we had real numbers.

People say everything's negotiable. Well, I'm here to tell you that the gas station attendant was not amused when I flung open the door and hollered, "It's been a tough month! How about I pay you cash and you knock two-thirds off my bill? Plus I'll throw in this coupon for some free wings at Applebee's."

You trim the variable costs—food, gasoline, car maintenance, personal waxing. You find ways to save or go without. You embrace thrift and discover the high of a true bargain. These aren't bad things; once you get past the learning curve, you actually start to curse yourself for all the money you'd wasted before. Meanwhile, thanks to unemployment insurance, our income had dropped by only two-thirds instead of three-thirds. I don't know what we'd have done without it. If I didn't find a job in the next couple of months, though, we were going to find out. Good thing I'd been stockpiling food like a deranged squirrel in yoga pants.

This was the first time I'd collected unemployment benefits so I wasn't sure what to expect, but it wasn't bad—the people at our Department of Labor want to help you find work. It also gave me a chance to get to know my community members better. I had been driving out of town at sunup and back into town at sundown, which hadn't left much time for socializing.

Hanging out at the Department of Labor changed that. Before Congress and the president cut a deal extending unemployment for deadbeats like me, I paid what I had thought was my last visit to the DoL office for a farewell party for some of us long-termers. There were party hats, noisemakers, and cake. They'd gone all out providing three kinds—chocolate for the transplants, red velvet for the real Southerners, and a carrot cake for the hippies. It sat forlornly on the edge of the table next to the crudités, ignored while we gluttonous slackers attacked the hot wings and store-brand potato chips with gusto.

I never did find the alleged beer cooler, but a guy offered me his flask of moonshine. I don't drink after people, not even my husband or children, but since we were talking serious alcohol here, I figured whatever crud that guy had left on the flask's rim wouldn't do me any lasting damage.

I took a furtive sip. The security guard was there performing his normal duties—holding up the wall next to the check-in and tidying up after ill-mannered clients stood to lumber after their counselors into the cubicle maze without taking a moment to shove in their chairs. A client suggested he give us all a pat down so we could pretend we were traveling somewhere by plane for the holidays. The security guard told the guy to pipe down and have some raw vegetables because that might be the last fresh veggies he sees for a while.

Some folks pocketed food. I looked away to give them their dignity and cursed myself for not carrying baggies with me.

The benefits were extended, but they were going to run out for me before the end of the year. I'll tell you—I would never have thought I'd be measuring unemployment in years instead of weeks or, at the most, a couple of months.

For a person like me, the jobs weren't there anymore. I applied for anything and everything. A friend in HR told me that employers were using all kinds of methods to winnow their applicant pools: your old salary compared with what they were willing to pay, employment status, length of unemployment, and credit checks.

That would have been swell if I'd been currently employed and making a decent but not too good salary and hadn't been flagged on my credit report for late payments for everything from overdue library fees to orthodontist bills.

While I surfed the Internet chasing jobs, my subconscious was tearing its hair out and wailing, *If you think this is bad, just imagine what things will be like when you're making nothing.* My subconscious was right to panic; we'd got a taste of zero income reality after a mix-up with my unemployment benefits.

January is already tough for a teacher's family. Starting in November, education people get their monthly paychecks early so they can blow them on restoratives like alcohol and at the mall on Black Friday. The December check arrives early and the next thing you know, you've landed headfirst in January, living on ramen noodles, stale oyster crackers, leftover candy canes, and those creamer thingies your kids steal from Waffle House. You're heating your house with the grill and seven-year-old Martha Stewart for Kmart hardwood charcoal you found in the bottom of a container in the shed. Good thing you were out there moving stuff around to put away the holiday decorations.

OK, I exaggerate. It's not *that* bad. If you're smart, you've paid most of the bills so you still have electricity, and the porn subscriptions are paid up. You've got your priorities.

But one day, I realized that the weekly deposit into my checking account was missing and the $8.33 my husband had paid for his monthly education society dues had morphed through the miracle of overdraft protection into $41.33. I visited the Department of Labor's website to see what the problem was, but all I got was a message telling me to report to my nearest DoL office. It was late, so I called the next morning and received the same response: "You have to come in to the office. We can't address these things over the phone due to privacy..." She sounded like she wanted to help, but her hands were tied.

I tried again. "I don't suppose whining about not having a car to get there today will change your answer?"

"Sorry, no. We get lots worse than whining. We can take it."

"I figured. I'll see you on Monday then. I'll be the woman with the haunted look who is chewing her hair."

"That's not much to go on considering the way things are here. Better wear a carnation so I can pick you out. We open at 7:30. Try not to worry too much."

Easy for her to say; she had a paycheck. I thanked her, hung up, snorted a line of confectioners' sugar, and got back to work looking for a job.

That Sunday, Georgia was hit with a snowstorm that resulted in not just a snow day, but a snow week. The Department of Labor finally opened on Wednesday and I made it in to say Hey, answer a few questions, and exchange a high five with my counselor, who was glad to be back at work after having been snowbound for two days with her own kids and a shortage of toilet paper.

I left with an eleven-week reprieve from financial doom. That meant more time to look for a job or to win the lottery.

As I was driving home, I was thinking about what an Eeyore I'd become. I wrote about being unemployed; I talked about it; when people asked how I was, I answered, "Still unemployed!" If I'd had disposable income, I would have had it tattooed on me somewhere.

This realization distressed me—I'd never identified with Eeyore! I saw myself as a charming mix of Tigger's exuberance and Pooh's steady cheerfulness with dashes of equal parts Piglet's anxieties and Rabbit's control issues and subcutaneous rage.

Come to think of it, I should have had a pink bow tattooed to my tail because I *was* Eeyore.

My mind wandered. A better person would have said that, after all, it's only money; it's not life or death, tragedy or sorrow. It's inconvenient and stressful, but it will pass and be replaced with a good day followed by other good days and occasional bad days.

Every one of those days was a chance to be better, to be Pooh or Tigger, Piglet or Rabbit.

Instead, I was entertaining myself by creating a backstory for the Winnie the Pooh characters. Pooh was cheerful because he smoked weed. Tigger's energy came from a raging coke habit that he supported by "bouncing" in alleys for money. Piglet popped Xanax like candy. Rabbit was a gambler and occasional huffer of cleaning supplies. And Eeyore? A total wino, of course.

QUICKIE from Susan:

I remember the time I was poor and semi-jobless. I was separated with no spousal support and couldn't pay the bills on my part-time salary. Then I discovered pure joy and total culinary bliss. It's called an EBT card, people, and that plastic thing can sure put some mighty delicious morsels on the table. We'd never eaten so good in all of our lives.

When I married a lawyer, I missed my EBT, once called food stamps but now designed to look like an ATM card to prevent embarrassment. We also qualified during that year for free lunches at the public schools. My kids actually thought that was cool, but I know in my day, I'd have been so mortified I'd have skipped lunch.

Sometimes, though, being poor isn't all that bad. Now that I have money, I can't wildly toss any and everything into my grocery cart. But at least if my husband leaves me, my old true love, Crown Prince EBT, will come dashing back into my life. I can smell the tender filet and wild-caught salmon on the grill as I type.

*When **Lisa Golden** began blogging, she assumed the persona of a political blogger in a lacy black bra. In a classic bait and switch, she began a series titled Adventures in Real Parenting and found that, much to her surprise, some of her readers actually remained.*

Mining her family's situation as part of the growing former American middle class for humor, she wrote her way through two long years of unemployment.

Away from the tyranny of the written word, Lisa plays the part of a cheerful eccentric with a recently acquired office job, three imperfect teen and young adult children, a quartet of politically active cats, an overdrawn bank account, and a flaming addiction to sugar.

Her husband plays her straight man when he's not threatening to teach her calculus against her will.

If you believe anonymous blog commenters, she's just another boring blogger who thinks she's creative, but until they take away her laptop, Lisa will continue to bore the readers of her blog That's Why, most of whom come around to comfort themselves with the knowledge that, no matter how bad their lot in life, at least they aren't her.

One Hundred Days of Solitude

by Bob Woodiwiss

Day 1: I am alone. Abandoned. Mateless. The Partner, a successful consultant to large corporations in need of role models for their unsuccessful consultants, left a few hours ago for a "short term out-of-town assignment." Translation: for the next four months, she'll be working and living in a city over 2,500 miles away. Her demanding schedule, she informs me, will not permit weekend returns home; likewise, my profound fear of flight attendants will preclude me from traveling to visit her. "This will be a long separation, but I shall endure it," she told me on her way out the door. I had to laugh, though, because in her clearly distracted state she'd said "enjoy" instead of "endure."

Day 8: What a week! Normally, when The Partner's around (and she's been around since my emergence from a protracted cannabis haze back in 1986, perhaps before; I really should ask), the words, "You're," "such," "a," and "pig" often come up, usually, though not always, in that order. I suspect this is because she still blames me for our last struggle with hookworms. (A war we eventually won but which cost us dearly in reparations.) Now, though, with no fussy female oversight, I'm allowing myself to devolve into man's primal state: unshaven; unchanged under-wear; un-plated, handheld meals; and fine, fluent, unapologetic ,flatulence. I'm feeling natural, undomesticated, liberated. Call me Sasquatch with HBO.

Day 19: It never occurred to me how difficult, how exhausting it would be to take care of our dog by myself. The greedy beast needs two daily walks, two daily feedings, two daily teeth brush-ings, grooming, countless trips outside to "feel the crapture," and frequent applications of Just for Men on his graying muzzle (his aging has us both rattled). He sorely misses The Partner, or as he sees her, the alpha female. Just this morning, he remarked, "I sorely miss the alpha female." Normally, I'd consider a talking dog quite extraordinary but not today; I happen to know the par-rot is working on its ventriloquist act.

Day 29: Irresponsibility, excess, and indulgence are transform-ing my body from temple to crack house. Consider: I haven't had a salad or lean meat for four weeks. Fruit is not even a household rumor. Yet I deny myself no fat or sweet. Dishes such as deep-fried salami and half-gallon bricks of ice cream hollowed into bowls then filled with cherry vodka are practically staples. All in all, this casting off of the shackles of nutrition and moderation feels redemptive, empowering; should I ever muster the will to stand up again, I'll quite possibly conquer the world.

Day 35: My father, knowing I'm alone and at loose ends, phones almost daily, urging me to visit. The fact that he's been dead for fifteen years tells me two things: (1) extended isolation is causing me to lose touch with reality, and (2) the dead know how to wangle a person's unlisted number.

Day 48: With The Partner, my muse, gone, I'm unfocused and can no longer write my normal 2,000 words a day. This is less seri-ous than it sounds since my home office gets very little walk-in traffic and I rarely sell more than a couple dozen overripe, deeply discounted adverbs in any given week. Still, in preparation for the time I'm able to resume my word output, I'm plugging away, typing in advance all the punctuation marks I'll eventually need.

Day 57: To maintain some intellectual engagement, I've begun visiting a Spanish language chat room. But it's difficult to make myself understood due to my poor written accent.

Day 66: Talked to The Partner on the phone today. She said I sounded good. "Good as compared to better or best?" I asked. "Or good as opposed to evil?" "Good as in 2,500 miles away," she responded.

Day 82: I've been on an inexplicable crying jag for three days. Inexplicable because the tears are streaming, somehow, from a location below my waist.

Day 90: I've decided this might be a good time to get together with my old army buddies for a poker game. To my dismay, regular GI Joe accuses GI Joe with Kung Fu Grip of cheating and, in a rage, melts him in the microwave.

Day 101: A few weeks ago, in a weak, desperate, sex-starved moment, I sent away for a Philippine mail-order bride. Today, she finally arrived on my doorstep, dead, suffocated by the bubble wrap she'd been packed in.

Day 111: In anticipation of The Partner's return, I engage a cleaning crew to tackle the squalor. They accept the job only after I take out a rider on my health insurance to cover them in case of cholera. As for my personal condition, the mirror reveals several gained pounds; I rate my grooming somewhere between chaotic and tragic. That showers and laundry have been infrequent undertakings would be obvious to all but the wholly noseless. The cumulative effect is that I appear to have had an extreme makeover in reverse. I drive to the dry cleaners and have myself Martinized.

Day 112: The Partner has returned. She says she's glad to be back. Says she missed her home, her routine. Says it's good to see me, to hold me, to kiss me. Says she wants a cracker. Only then do I realize the parrot is practicing his act again.

Bob Woodiwiss *writes a humor column for* Cincinnati Magazine *and is a regular contributor to* McSweeney's Internet Tendency. *He is the author of* Keys to Uncomfortable Living: An Indulgence of My Peculiarities, An Indictment of Yours, *and his work is included in* The McSweeney's Book of Politics and Musicals. *He is also the owner of and Director of Undirected Thinking at Bob, The Agency, a creative boutique. Look for him sitting alone on a couch at parties or follow him on Twitter @bwsez.*

Battle of the Naked Zydeco Bands

by Del Shannon

As we pulled into the Rosie Cheeks nudist community parking lot Beth, my wife, said, "You're going to keep your clothes on."

"Of course," I answered as I parked the car and turned off the engine.

"No," she continued, grabbing my chin and yanking my face in front of hers, trying to tunnel her point into my brain. "Just because we're going to nudist camp doesn't mean you have to get naked." One of these days I've got to figure out exactly how she gets inside my head.

"OK, OK," I mumbled.

"We're just here to see John and Maureen's zydeco band. They begged and we promised, but that's it. There will be no sympathetic naked participation. Got it?"

"How do you come up with the idea to start a naked zydeco band?" I asked, trying to distract her, as we walked toward the entrance.

"How do you do anything naked?" Beth answered as we walked. "Wait, don't answer that. I know what you're thinking." How does she do that?

"I will tell you that's the last time I have four margaritas at any dinner they're at," she grumbled.

The dance hall wasn't difficult to find. Indiscernibly blaring music and a small crowd of naked people very carefully smoking cigarettes outside a large white building just to the right of the entrance told us exactly where we needed to go. Already I could tell Beth was getting queasy with the whole naked thing.

"There's going to be quite a bit of that tonight. Better try and get used to it," I mumbled while nodding in the direction of the naked loiterers.

"I know," she hissed back. "It's just...well, some people shouldn't be naked in front of other naked people. What if someone gets," she paused for the right word, "interested, in someone else tonight."

I looked at the group of baby-suited smokers. "No chance anyone's going to get 'interested' in that group," I offered and tried to focus on getting into the building without saying something I'd regret later on.

I'm not sure what I expected to see, this being my first time inside a nudist camp. But I can tell you I didn't expect to see our friends, John and Maureen, jumping, naked, around on the stage playing and singing Louisiana swamp music. Maureen had warned me about the custom washboard she used, the one with two cutouts conveniently placed in its front, but I still wasn't ready for the actual sight of...them.

She was scratching the front of the washboard (scritcha-scratcha, scritcha-scratcha) while her two accompanists thwacked away on the offbeat with her strategically timed jumps and dives. Scritcha-scratcha, thwacka-thwacka. Scritcha-scratcha, thwacka-thwacka. John was sucking away on a harmonica but, while he looked like he was having a good time, his body language suggested he was very uninterested.

Beth was wide-eyed at the whole scene and I could tell she was becoming a little too fixated on John. "He's probably just a little nervous...or cold," I offered in defense of the entire male species. "It's no big deal," I continued, instantly regretting my choice of words.

And then the song ended and we suddenly realized we were standing in the middle of the room staring slack jawed like idiots, except completely clothed idiots. Quickly recovering, we scurried to an empty table and sat down. A minute later, we caught John and Maureen's eyes and they quickly scurried over and sat down next to us. "You two been here long?" John asked.

"Just got here," I said, trying to keep my eyes locked on their faces. "Sorry we're late. Sitter," I offered with a shrug.

"That's OK, you caught our big finale," Maureen said with a giggle. "I'm sure we'll win the Battle of Naked Zydeco Bands if we can just beat this next act, Jim's Big Band."

Jim had a full naked band behind him but his instrument was, like Maureen's, a custom built washboard with a small cymbal hanging off the bottom. Jim's Big Band jumped immediately into what sounded like a zydeco standard with Jim jumping around the stage and scritcha-scratching away just like Maureen.

After several songs that mostly sounded exactly the same, I had to admit that the thwacka-thwacka of Maureen's washboard had me sold on her band as the winner...until Jim started using his cymbal. Right in the middle of their last song, like a bolt from the blue, Jim gave a little oomph from downtown and clanged that cymbal on the offbeat. The place went nuts. Scritcha-scratcha, clang. Scritcha-scratcha, clang.

"Maybe we should start having you play the washboard?" Maureen groaned to John as she saw another missed opportunity to win the Battle of the Naked Zydeco Bands slip away. But then, after a long pause, and a discreet look, she said with a short sigh, "Or maybe not."

Beth and I stayed for the awards ceremony and cheered thunderously for John and Maureen's second place trophy, like the good friends we are. But it wasn't until the ride home that Beth finally came clean. "You know, I think the Simons have one of those old washboards."

"No!" I barked.

"And Alex has that cheap drum set he got for Christmas when he was three," she continued.

"There will be no cymbal playing with parts of the body that shouldn't be playing the cymbal," I said, vigorously continuing my defense.

"You're such a weenie," she said with a smile.

"OK, that's not fair," I said. "Yes, I'm a weenie, but not in the way you're thinking." We rode the rest of the way home with her calling me a weenie and me secretly thanking God Almighty that I was, indeed, a world-class weenie.

Del Shannon is a full-time civil engineer who designs and constructs (and sometimes even deconstructs) dams around the world. He is also a writer. When not working on dams, he has written award-winning essays, newspaper columns, and children's stories. In 2007, he received the Erma Bombeck Humor Writing Award for his humorous essay "Republican Hair." His first children's book was the serialized novella The Map, *published in several newspapers. His second children's book and first full-length novel,* Captain Disaster, *is currently with several editors-at-large and important-sounding publishing houses. He lives with his family in Colorado, plays intramural soccer on three different teams, and always seems to be daydreaming.*

Investment Banking

by Joel Schwartzberg

Jennie had clear skin, ocean-blue eyes, and an acrylic nametag that read, simply, "Jennie." From where I stood in line, the bank's fluorescent lights bounced magically off her golden hair. I imagined her wearing suede boots, but of course there was no way of knowing—the counter was chest-high, and there was that bulletproof glass partition.

Recently freed from college, I was spending nights on a friend's cat-urine-stained futon, earning a biweekly check doing freelance jobs for Dick Clark's production company. At the time, I yearned for anything to which I could anchor my life; and in my twenty-two-year-old mind, nothing was more grounding than a capital-G girlfriend.

So when Jennie called out to me from behind that counter—to untrained ears, it simply sounded like "next"—I floated toward her and presented my check.

"Are you in the entertainment industry," she said, thumbing the embossed Dick Clark Productions logo. Her fingernails were fire-truck red.

"Yes."

"Do you know Dick Clark?"

"I see him from time to time," I said. This was true enough; I've caught many glimpses of Dick Clark walking from his office to the limousine.

"How do you want it?"

I blinked.

"Tens and twenties OK?"

"Sure." I would have been OK with singles, pesos, euros, cattle...

I wasn't holding up my end of the conversation. Too busy with the parallel-world conversation in my head, the one in which we were nearly engaged.

And then, just like that, the ride was over. There were bills in my hand.

Jennie's big eyes met mine. "Thanks, and come again."

Come again. That was nice.

As we parted ways, I felt her warm eyes follow me. Or maybe they'd just turned off the air conditioning.

Two weeks later, I returned to the bank with swollen confidence and ironed jeans. I'd brought a personal check of my own as an icebreaker. It wasn't from Dick Clark, but it would have to do.

But there was no line. I could see Jennie casually playing with her hair, waiting for attention. It was all happening too soon. I nodded to the security guard. I read a brochure about home equity loans. I killed some time at the ATM. Nervous, I accidentally double-pressed the zero and withdrew $200 instead of $20. I didn't even think I had $200.

There was a short line now, and I took my place. Jennie was serving a pudgy man in cargo pants. I planned my openings:

"Tens would be fine. So would your phone number..."

"How about you help me spend this..."

"I don't usually ask out complete strangers, but..."

The line moved well, but Cargo Pants apparently had all the time in the world, and was still chatting up my Jennie. Jesus, was he withdrawing his entire account in nickels? Making a third world debt repayment? Or was he focusing his squinty eyes on her and saying, *"I don't usually ask out complete strangers, but..."*

At this rate, my trajectory would have put me in the care of a stick-figured woman named Lupina. When you're in a service line—whether at the bank or at McDonald's—it's one thing to predict your teller and quite another to manipulate the natural order of fate. I let a hefty woman in a polyester sweater pass ahead of me, then sized up the business suit behind me.

I looked back at the counter, and Cargo Pants was gone. And instead of heading for Lupina, Polyester was beelining toward Jennie. I grabbed her by the shoulder.

"Mind if I go ahead? She's...she's my sister."

Though clearly confused, Polyester just nodded. I trotted toward Jennie, holding the check out like a golden ticket.

"Hi," Jennie said.

Hi is miles from *Hello*. Everyone knows that.

"I'm cashing this, please... Jennie."

I swallowed hard as she punched up my account.

"Listen," I said, at first looking at my fingers. "I don't usually do this, but...would you be interested in the idea of maybe having dinner on me? I mean, *with* me. With me. But still, on me, of course. Maybe we can go to that new French place, Liaison Paris?"

Jennie scrunched her eyes at her screen.

"I'm flattered, but I don't think so."

I wasn't about to give up.

"I know we hardly know each other, but we're practically neighbors. I thought we hit it off last time talking about Dick Clark and the...you know, tens and twenties..."

"I don't mean to embarrass you, but are you sure you can afford it?"

A bead of sweat dripped down the side of my T-shirt.

"Hmm?"

"I can't cash your check. Insufficient funds to cover." She looked at her screen. "According to this, I think you owe *us* money."

I felt twenty-two pairs of eyes on me, and there were only six people in the bank. Dick Clark had left the building.

"Owe you money? No, there's a mistake. A rounding error. You're in finance. You understand."

No more than two minutes later, I was outside the bank. And like a successful robber, I knew I could never return. The next closest bank branch was miles away, but I made the trek from then on, knowing I couldn't step into Jennie's branch for the rest of my life or until I had facial reconstructive surgery, whichever came first.

If you've ever changed banks before, you know it's no picnic. But two things made it easier: One was direct deposit. The other was a raven-haired young woman who worked at the new accounts desk and smelled like flowers. She gave me a free magnet. I think her name was Mia.

A nationally published essayist, public speaking coach, Internet executive, law school dropout, and doomed Wheel of Fortune *contestant,* **Joel Schwartzberg** *is the author of the personal essay collection* The 40-Year-Old Version *(www.bookfordad.com), which won first place in the humor category of the 2010 Next Generation Indie Book Awards, and second place in the humor category of the 2010 ForeWord Book of the Year Awards.*

Joel's work has appeared in Newsweek, The New York Times Magazine, The New York Daily News, The New York Post, New Jersey Monthly, The Star-Ledger, Chicken Soup for the Soul, Babble.com, *PBS Parents,* The Huffington Post, The Good Men Project, AOL ParentDish, *and in regional parenting magazines across the US and Canada.*

A father to three, husband to one, and slave to six cats, Joel can be reached through his portfolio at www.joelschwartzberg.net.

Shock and Soy Sauce

by Kim Bongiorno

One typical Friday night I found myself on the couch, stroking my cats while eating out of a box of Cap'n Crunch. Before turning on the TV, I asked my brother if he cared whether I put on the PJs that had the hole in the crotch. His silent expression was all I needed to see: It was time to start dating again.

As it happened, my best friend had called me up out of the blue to insist that I go on my very first blind date with a doctor from her office. She gave me all sorts of pinky swears that he was the Full Package. She and I have been best friends since we were fifteen. We knew each other better than anyone else, and I trusted her judgment.

The guy who rang my bell that January night wasn't as handsome as described, but considering I was close to becoming the crazy cat lady, I couldn't complain. I had been running late, and apologized that I needed him to wait a few minutes while I got ready. He was patient and understanding. I ducked into my bedroom and locked the door.

What followed was a series of clangs, shuffles, door slams, and thunks from the other room that confused me greatly. I had three pieces of furniture in my tiny living room—what could he possibly be doing in there?

I was stuffing a lip gloss into my purse as I exited my bedroom telling him I was ready to go. When I looked up, he was standing in the center of my living room with a grin on his face, surrounded by a guitar, amp, microphone stand, music stand, and song lyrics.

What. The HELL.

He threw up his hands, exclaiming "Surprise!" which was less an understatement and more of an inaccurate synonym for "insane." I couldn't quite form the obvious question, so he explained that my friend had mentioned at one point that I could sing and that he was not going to leave my home until I performed a song for him.

Sure, I had a habit of singing in the shower, but this didn't qualify me for one-woman shows. In my living room. On a first date.

"Uh. I. Don't. Sing."

"Don't be modest, c'mon. I even brought you music."

I walked over to the music stand (who the hell carries a music stand around?), curiosity getting the better of me, to read the title of the song he had at the ready for me: "Luka" by Suzanne Vega.

Oh, the song about child abuse? How romantic.

The genuine smile on his face would have been adorable had he just not filled my apartment with concert paraphernalia and asked me to sing the words of a child who gets beat up every night. Reminding myself that surely my best friend would not have sent a psychopath to my home, I said, "I'm not singing, I'm going to dinner. With or without you," and headed out the door.

He chased me, and offered to drive us to the restaurant.

I wasn't even buckled in before this dashing chatterbox noted what a coincidence it was that we happened to drive the same Volkswagen Jetta, though mine was white and his was black.

"How can you afford it?"

After a *Did he really just ask me that?* breath, I replied, "I have a job. It earns me money to pay for things like rent, food, and a car."

"Wow, it's just...Jettas are really expensive. How much do you make?"

He knows we have Jettas, not Porches...right?

"Enough."

"How much exactly?"

"I just met you. I'm not telling you how much money I make."

"Well! You don't have to get snippy about it."

I appreciated his pouty silence for the next few minutes of the ride.

As he pulled into the parking lot of a Japanese restaurant he insisted was the best around, he began spewing his unsolicited opinion on every eating establishment he thought didn't live up to its hype. He considered himself a foodie with a gifted palate, and his good opinion was hard to win.

As scintillating as this one-way conversation was, I found myself thinking fondly of my lumpy couch and stash of TV dinners.

Since it was early January, I was carefully traversing the slick blacktop while dispensing *"mmhmm"*s as we headed into the restaurant when suddenly his throaty pontifications were interrupted by a girlish shriek and him throwing himself at the mercy of my left arm.

Dude almost knocked me to the ground and then proceeded to put most of his weight on me for the duration of the journey, all the while peppering every other step with a squeal of terror. My Nana was easier to help across black ice than this guy.

I forced myself not to roll my eyes while holding the door for Prince Slipperyshoes and stepped inside the quiet restaurant. As I'd expected, I was clueless when I looked over the menu. As the one who was familiar with Japanese offerings, he asked my likes and dislikes, then placed our order. It was hard to find footing in conversation, being that since the only things he wanted to talk about were my 401K balance and how he can tell exactly which kinds of sashimi are in a rainbow roll on the first bite—I was happy for the distraction of our drinks and appetizers.

My date wouldn't let the server tell me what we were eating, and after a quick (concerned?) look, the woman stepped away. I thought he was trying to make a gesture, walking me through the experience of trying Japanese food for the first time. Determined to make the best of this night, I went along. This is when he asked me a simple question while fiddling with his chopsticks: "Do you like spicy foods?"

"Sure. I like Mexican food, and as long as it's not too hot."

My eyes landed upon a curious chartreuse blob of goo on the edge of his plate that he was scraping into one big dime-sized ball. It looked smooth and firm, like a kind of butter. He smiled as he picked it up with his chopsticks.

"Then open up."

This was a bit too intimate for my tastes, but it wasn't like the guy licked the chopsticks before trying to feed me. I accepted the pretty green ball.

About five seconds later, I was screaming f-bombs across the restaurant.

He had fed me wasabi, which is essentially like tossing a fistful of flame down an innocent woman's throat. I gagged, fighting back vomit. I yelled in his face, and threw a glass of water into my mouth as tears streamed down my cheeks.

I gasped for breath, shouting, "WHY WOULD YOU DO THAT TO ME?"

He shrugged while I clawed at my tongue to scrape off any remaining horror paste. "I thought you'd like it?"

"Bullshit!" I gulped down another glass, noticing the family with kids next to us. "Sorry! BUT MY DATE JUST POISONED ME WITH GREEN FIRE."

I sucked my beer down in one swoop, then called the waiter over for more water or bread or a fire extinguisher.

I figured my mascara was creating a Rorschach test across my pale face, so I gently swiped at the tears, effectively depositing sizzling beads of wasabi into my eyes.

"OH MY GOD, MY EEEEEEEEYES!" I shoved my cloth napkin into his glass of water and started rubbing my burning eyes. As droplets splayed across the table, I asked him what was wrong with him, in much more colorful language than one should use in the middle of a public restaurant.

In a small voice, he calmly whispered, "I really think you're overreacting."

I hate you. I hate you. I. HATE. YOU.

I pulled the sopping-wet, make-up-smeared napkin from my face. Damp tendrils of hair stuck up haphazardly in a crown of shock. "Over. *Reacting?*"

As bad as it was, I knew I couldn't leave. My best friend worked with this idiot every day, and as much as I wanted to cause him the same physical pain as he caused me, I couldn't do anything to make her work environment uncomfortable. So I did what anyone would do in this situation: I ran the tab up as high as it could possibly go.

I ordered a massive bowl of rice to extinguish the fire in my belly, and as many expensive bland things as I could, daring him with my furrowed brow to tell me to stop. I ate until I was full to bursting, and asked for the check before the Dimwit of Dining Destruction ordered some Grasshopper Cake with Habañero Colon Blow Hot Sauce Frosting for dessert.

Take that, you Jetta-driving jackass.

He practically wept as he paid the inflated bill, and we silently headed home. At the end of my street, he brought up how my friend had told him that I was a rock climber. I confirmed that, yes, I was.

He shook his head, and said just couldn't believe a girl could do something like that.

Whoever said "Boys are stupid. Throw rocks at them." was totally onto something.

I pinched the spot between my eyebrows and begged for Zen. This guy needed to come inside to collect his jam session apparatus. I wondered if I had the strength to not punch him in the spleen before he left. I persevered.

Once inside, he asked me again whether I was sure I couldn't sing just once verse of "Luka." The answer was very clearly no, so he quickly removed all his musical crap. When he was done, he said my friend told him I had a great rock climbing photo album, then stood there, waiting.

Note to self: Leave a horse head made of wasabi in my friend's bed while she's sleeping the next time I'm in town.

I sighed, slid it off the shelf, and sat down with him, as he looked it over. After each of the 200 photographs he said, "Wow. You really are a rock climber. You climb rocks. This is you climbing. Man, that's a real mountain. You have rock climbing gear." Over and over again, like the delightful conversationalist I had dreamed of meeting all those lonely nights.

97

Finally, we got to the last page in the album. He snapped it shut and stood. Not one to pass up an opportunity to kick an asshat out of my home, I stood with him and opened my mouth to say, "Well, it's been a real hoot. Let's call it a night," but he suddenly grabbed my forearms, pulled me in, and dry-mouth kissed me without moving for just short of an eternity. My baby powder–scented elderly aunts kissed with more passion than this guy.

He pulled away, and smiled while saying, "Well. I guess we'll never do *this* again" and walked out of my apartment.

I blinked a few times at the quiet room, wondering if that all had really just happened. The vague burning sensation still blurring my vision confirmed that it did. Within minutes I was in a long hot shower washing off the odor of shock and soy sauce that lingered on my skin, vowing to never say to myself again:

"It's just a blind date. How bad could it possibly be?"

It can be A Fist of Wasabi in the Eye bad. *That's* how bad a blind date can be.

QUICKIE from DC:

I have plenty of stories about really bad dates, but nearly being blinded by a blind date—with a condiment—is one of a kind. During my twenties, I lived in Dallas and loitered around a comedy club so frequently that I became good friends with the bartenders; most of the time I drank for free. I was also kind of a comic groupie, and dated a few of the comedians. I went out with, and sometimes stayed in with, Jim O'Brien, the sighted half of the O'Brien and Valdez comedy team. Jim asked me if I had a friend for Alex—so that we could double date. My friend Jamie was a good sport to let me fix her up on a blind date, with a blind guy.

Kim Bongiorno *is a writer, blogger, mother of two, and wife look-ing at her suburban life and wondering what the hell just happened. Her blog,* **Let Me Start By Saying…,** *earned her a spot as a Circle of Moms Top 25 Funny Mom in 2011 and 2012 and has received the accolades of sites such as* Babble, HuffPostParents, NickMom, *and* BlogHer. *When not sharing inappropriately amusing lists on her blog or shock-ing the innocent in a weekly humor column at* InThePowderRoom, *Kim can be found tweaking her young adult novel's manuscript and finding ways to convince her husband it's OK to spend endless hours on Facebook.*

Anastasia Steele Was Clearly Not a Mother of Three

by Brittany Gibbons

Having been married for somewhere between seven and a hundred thousand years, there are some basic logistical facts that I know to be true. You won't have sex as often as you did in college; without surgery, your boobs become as aesthetically pleasing as a couple of handbags; and after expelling their fair share of children, your vagina and abdomen wave their white flags in surrender.

As unappealing as that all sounds, none of it will probably have any bearing on whether or not your husband wants to have sex with you. To him, you're as lovely and sexually capable, if not more, than you were the day he married you, and marital sex has become no less of an adventure no matter how many new jiggly parts he has to hold on to.

The problem, then, lies with me. Mentally, intercourse has become more taxing, what with all the to-lists and dance recitals and soccer games and overdraft fees. Enjoyable sex occurs somewhere in my brain, and when I can't get that part firing on all mental cylinders, I'm basically just a limp hole, lying on the mattress going over the next day's work deadlines until he's finished and collapsed on top of me.

Fifty Shades of Questionably Edited Erotica has opened my mind to a whole new realm of stimulation, making sex a mostly two-sided, mutually climaxing affair. It's like foreplay for my brain, shutting off all the noise and reminding me that sometimes, all I need is a spanking or two.

Sure, there are a lot of things about the series that are downright preposterous. Christian can have sex sixty times in a row? Nobody showers afterward, they just walk around with sex stink, and UTIs don't exist? People still own teacups?

While I found the overall premise of the books to be about as believable as Donatella Versace's breasts, face, and lips, one aspect did intrigue me a bit: the Ben Wa balls.

Except not in an *Oh, those look orgasmic!* way but more like an, *Oh, those might make me stop peeing all over myself!* way.

Because after three back-to-back kids my vaginal walls are broken; they just sit there all frowny and let shit like urine and tampons just fall out. They look like those *Sesame Street* Martians that discover mundane objects.

I've tried doing Kegel exercises, but they give me headaches. Flexing that muscle makes my forehead crunch up and my top lip go numb, and then my head starts to hurt. Maybe I'm doing it wrong?

Anyway, Ben Wa balls are also supposed to help tighten those muscles, and, unlike the electric ab belt that was supposed to shock my stomach into a six-pack, I figured this was would be at least marginally more effective and probably less flammable. (On the plus side, though, I no longer have a happy trail.)

I did my research and decided on Smartballs because they're connected to each other and have a string that hangs outside your body. My doctor *insists* that things can't get lost in my vagina and float up to my brain, but he's apparently never had to fish out a lost tampon string while squatting over his grandfather's toilet in the middle of August.

So I bought these Smartballs, which look way bigger in real life, to force my birth canal to be less canal-y and more trickling brook-y; and if it also resulted in better sex, wonderful! Although in general, I'm an outside sex enjoyer, not an inside sex enjoyer… *if you know what I mean.*

The instructions say to just put a little lube on them, shove them up there, and then go about your everyday activity while they strengthen your pelvic floor.

I decided to plop them in one afternoon and Incredible Hulk my cookie while I folded laundry and my husband, Andy, napped. They went in super easy, but when I went to walk out of the bathroom, they slipped right out and fell on the tile. *Obviously,* I must have put them in incorrectly. I pushed the balls back in and then carefully made my way to the basket of clothes on the bed.

I folded everything, putting it into neat piles, thighs squeezed tightly together so the balls could get some muscle work done. It wasn't until I moved to start hanging clothes in the closet that things went awry.

With each step, they slowly began to peek out, so I closed my thighs together and decided to just make my way to the closet using a series of choreographed calf movements. It looked weird, but it would be worth it when I could Dougie without peeing my pants.

Uh-oh.

"What are you doing?"

"What?"

"Why are you walking like that? What's wrong with your legs?"

"Nothing. Go back to sleep."

"Seriously, what are you doing?"

"Nothing. God, stop stalking me, Andy."

"Just move your legs apart."

"You're a pervert."

"Move them."

"Uggghhhh." *weird puckering sound* *thud*

"Did you just shit on the floor?"

"No. Jesus. They're exercise balls, they fell out of my vagina. Do we have no boundaries anymore?"

Oh my. Looks like this whole thing is going to be less of a sprint and more of a teenager-trying-to-give-agonizingly-long,-slimy-birth–in-a-Walmart-bathroom marathon.

QUICKIE from Susan:

As you may or may not know, my family called the vagina the "possum" while my younger sister and I were growing up.

"Cross your legs, I can see your possum," Mama would say.

Or, "Cover up. You're taking my picture with that possum flashing. You're blinding me!"

Never would I think in a zillion years, I'd wake up one morning with TWO possums.

It all started when my entire vagina area fell from my pelvic floor like a drunk Randy Travis.

I had decided to run a 5k, and by the way, I do not run. Ever. After the race, I felt something weird emerging from between my legs, kind of like a ping-pong ball protrusion. Ick, but true.

I remembered that one of my aunts had had something fall out of her possum once. She'd called my mama frantically and said, "Get over here now and see what's coming out of me. It's big enough to do an old lady a lot of good."

She'd called it her mini-penis, but it was actually her bladder.

And that's what I saw when I looked into my Lancôme compact mirror: a big pink ball.

Long story short...I went to the doc, who told me that my bladder, uterus (aka "Bitch in a Bag"), and vaginal walls had prolapsed.

"How could they collapse?" I beseeched this possum-peeping professional. "I've only birthed one baby through the...the... Tunnel of Love, and the other was a C-section. All my boyfriends had tragically small penises. Like putt-putt pencils."

She grimaced and scheduled surgery. It was horrific.

Four days later, I felt some mystery lumps, and looked in the mirror only to discover four labia —a woman is supposed to have two. I had the "Double Possum Syndrome," and the doc immediately called in an arsenal of antibiotics to prevent further "spreadage" of my broken-down 'giner.

This reminded me of the complete shock I had experienced the time I decided to de-fur myself "down there." I'd had no idea a possum could look so...well...not-so-fetching. It did not help I'd used dog clippers to shave off all the mats and dreadlocks.

The good news is that the meds worked and I'm down to one set of outer labia. The bad news? The bladder fell again, and I have to have the entire surgery repeated.

This time, they're bringing out the big guns—that controversial sling that all the lawyers are making money from. But this means that if something else goes wrong with my possum, I'll at least get a nice income out of it.

Maybe if I somehow get some extra possum-age again, I can finally join the circus as the freak show attraction: "Pay $5 and see a real woman with TWO vaginas and a starter penis."

__Brittany Gibbons__ is a writer, humorist, and catalyst. Known for her satirical wit and self-deprecation, Brittany authors the award-winning humor blog BrittanyHerself.com, in which she over-shares bits of her life between phonetically spelled sound effects and excessive ellipses. She is also a ted speaker, a television personality, and the founder of the body image advocacy site CurvyGirlGuide.com

Open Letter to the Person Who Told My Mother Her Hair Looked Good this Way

by Lockie Hunter

Dear Idiot Who Told My Mother Her Hair Was Beautiful This Way,

Perhaps you could not anticipate that she would take your words with such gravity that her hairstyle would remain unchanged through Kennedy's untimely death, the tumultuous years of LBJ, the Nixon scandal, the lost years of Ford, the Reagan administration, the Clinton years, and now well into the Bushes' dynasty? Were you just being polite?

I ask you, honestly, Was this hairstyle ever in fashion? I cannot identify an era when it would have been leading edge. It is not mod. It is neither hep nor hip. It is neither punk nor conservative. It defies gravity and fingerprinting. Many have tried to characterize it and have become lost.

When Mother moves to a new city and is fated to seek a new stylist, she often asks that I— a woman teeming with words— tackle the job of describing her "do." I meekly cast it as a sort of a modified bob with a large clump teased onto the top, Westminster show-poodle fashion, the crowning touch of which is a large cone of swirled hair that resembles cotton candy. So much does this "crown" resemble cotton candy that it is reported that as a child I used to reach greedily for it and say "candy." Then the other adults would laugh with such force...So you, I hope you're happy.

Did you say something like, "This is your signature style" or "Don't ever change even when countless hairdressers, friends, and family advise you to change"? I noodle over what your exact words must have been; frankly, it keeps me up at night. I mean, what were you thinking? Was it an act of derring-do? Perhaps you were a little drunk that day? You'd had a morning highball for lunch?

Although, to her credit, Mother's hairstyle does add at least a foot to her stature. Being petite, she appreciates this. Every time we discuss her height, we add the phrase, "And with hair, why, she is at least five feet, three inches tall if she is an inch." Were you entered into some sort of cosmetologist hair height contest?

Did you tell her that this style was, and I quote, "lovely, simply lovely, why you're as pretty as a picture" as some sort of dare? Perhaps you were being sarcastic? This last scenario seems the most likely. You were being sarcastic in your "compliment" and Mother, being the unpresumptuous lady that she is, why she simply misunderstood is all. That "compliment" was an act of pure evil. Well I just hope you are pleased.

The good folks at BigHairDoCorp, owner of the Aqua Net hair spray brand send Mother a Christmas card each year, as she is the second largest buyer in the Upper Peninsula. Sadly, Mother may be personally responsible for well over 1/32 of the ozone depletion in her home state. Some estimates hold the figure at a full 1/16 percent. And, by association, you are responsible as well. Do you read the memorandums of the polar caps melting? There are entire islands that are at risk of being swallowed whole by the expanding ocean.

You are basically at fault. I hope you are satisfied.

QUICKIE from Susan:

Twice when I changed my hairdo and ran a new look in my newspaper column photo, I received death threats. "This hairstyle makes your nose dip into your lipstick like some sort of fishhook for catching the rarest of rainbow trout," the note said. "Your nose seems to have grown side wings, as well. It would be in your best interest to immediately change this horrific hairstyle. If not, I will personally take you and the stylist behind a barn and shoot you both."

As an aside, I had a boyfriend who dumped me when I dyed my hair crow black. Another ditched me when I got a perm. And still another wanted me to actually style my hair down there!

QUICKIE from DC:

I have a very thick mane, naturally curly and wild looking. I have tried to tame it down over the years by blow drying and flat ironing, but Mother Nature is inevitably my stylist. My hair could be Flat Stanley in the morning, and by noon on a humid summer day, it will be Three Stooges—Larry again (Curly was ironically named, as he had a buzz cut). My older sister Lori is quite a fashionista, and changes hairstyles so often that I wonder if she has a quota. On a girls' weekend at the lake, with ninety-degree temperatures and no air conditioning, the topic mysteriously switched from ex-husbands to my hair. (We never run out of ex-husband material.)

Lori: "Um, DC, you know you've had that same hairdo for fifteen years." Then, one by one, the other girls each commented. "Have you thought about cutting it?" "It's just sooo much hair." "Do you wear it like that for work, too?" "Straight hair is really popular right now." Me: "What the hell is this, a hair intervention?"

It was a hair intervention. Of all my questionable life choices throughout the years and of all the subjects friends and family might conspire to intervene in, this was about as obscure as a *fingernail intervention for Lindsay Lohan. On second thought, though, they did look really bad at her last trial...*

Into the Wild: Urban Cougars Pose New Threat to Kids

by Aimee Heckel

My elementary school not only had snow days. We also had cougar days.

Ah yes, childhood in the Colorado mountains. We treated the massive, bloodthirsty cats in our tree houses and on top of the gymnasium like we did natural disasters: with cautious respect. Teachers planned about ten cougar days a semester into the schedule; they were basically mountain holidays.

I remember one holiday in particular. It seemed like a regular day in music class, and then I heard it, a low growl outside. I was standing at the window on the second floor, and at my eye level in the top of a cottonwood tree clung a fat cat. Suddenly, the principal was on the intercom sending kids home, and I was home in time to watch *He-Man*. I was simultaneously elated and freaked out.

As a firsthand expert on the threat of cougars, I have been commissioned by myself to warn society about a new crop of cougars hunting kids across America: the urban cougars.

Following is all you need to know to stay safe in these trying times.

The urban cougar: A female *Homo sapiens* mammal, late thirties to fifty-five years old, known to prey on younger males, never older than twenty-five but typically older than elementary-school age.

Physical characteristics: The cougar has distinct markings that include leopard and/or zebra print, hot pink lace, and spiky hooves, also known as "stilettos." The cougar has a lean and agile body, useful for stalking and ambushing, as are her sharp, painted claws and aerodynamic sports car. The body of a cougar comprises at least 43 percent synthetic material—look for plastic enhancements near the chest, haunches, snout, jaws, claws, lips, and teeth. Owing to these artificial reinforcements, it is difficult to gauge the cougar's genetic age, and she's unlikely to tell you even if you ask her; experts recommend adding fifteen years to the year that her favorite song was released, twenty years if it's by Bruce Springsteen and she calls him "The Boss."

Other variations: "Cougar hunters" must take extra care not to confuse a cougar with one of its subspecies or the result could be disastrous.

First, there is the mountain lion. Although it shares the cougar's habitat, diet, and demeanor, the mountain lion's fur is highly processed, as well as twice as long and up to three times as poufy as cougars'. The mountain lion's skin is orange and of a leather or tree bark consistency. Also, upon careful inspection, you will see a discrepancy between the facial flesh (flawless beneath the Botox, foundation, night creams, and clothespins) and the dangling neck below (wrinkled with age rings, akin to the rings in a tree stump).

The puma, or cougar in training, is another variety. The puma exhibits early signs of cougar behavior, such as circling college campuses when hungry and wearing oversized sunglasses to hide eye wrinkles, except the puma is familiar with modern popular culture and has not been married more than three times.

Habitat: The cougar resides in big cities and hibernates year-round in tanning salons. When not holed up in the UV cave, cougars occupy one of two extremes during daylight hours: in an executive business post or as a stay-at-home wife or divorcee with what can only be called "mega alimony." At night, this chiefly nocturnal creature flocks to clubs, hotel bars, lounges, or dueling piano shows, but only ones with dim lighting—as bright light can spark a "Gremlins"-like episode.

Demeanor: Self-sufficient, focused, swift, goal-oriented, and noncommittal. Cougars are also shrewd and highly skilled hunters. If you're being pursued by a cougar, do not run or throw things; this can anger the animal and members of its ever nearby pack. Instead, it's safest to stay silent, close your eyes, and lie on the ground face-up. The cougar will then bat you around a bit, bite you, and vanish into the night air never to be seen again. A cougar will never capture the same prey twice.

Diet: Rose zinfandel, gin and tonic with a lime, lettuce and breath mints.

Popularity: Although cougars themselves do not breed to procreate, the population appears to be on the rise. Prominent leaders of the cougar clan include Samantha Jones of *Sex and the City*, Demi Moore, Susan Sarandon, and Naomi Watts. The term "cougar" has also appeared on shows such as *30 Rock* and in the movie *Ocean's Thirteen*. There was also NBC's reality dating show *Age of Love*, which pitted so-called kittens in their twenties against cougars in their forties. I am currently trying to get NBC to pick up my idea for another reality show: pitting urban cougars against hungry Rocky Mountain cougars in the hunt for a young, hot frat boy.

The battle would be intense, trust me. I recently had to call my own cougar day, right in downtown Denver.

I was out with my boyfriend. It seemed like a regular night, but then I heard it, building to a crescendo on the opposite side of the room: dueling pianos. Suddenly, the lights dimmed, the doors slammed shut, and I smelled it: self-tanner.

The bloodthirsty cats were out. Just like back in the day, these beasts were scoping out the nearby kids. And with a boyfriend in his early twenties, I knew we had to proceed with cautious respect.

I immediately called a cougar day, slamming my gin and tonic with a lime so we could go home to safety. I stood up, wobbling in my stilettos, and snatched my boyfriend with my sharp red claws, er, fingernails. Suddenly, it hit me: I was almost thirty, and I was totally wearing leopard print.

My boyfriend stayed silent as I slowly sat back down and ordered a zinfandel, rose. I think I saw him tremble a little, though whether in excitement or fear, I couldn't tell. It was too dark behind my huge sunglasses.

Aimee Heckel is a freak. She also writes an award-winning humor style column (turns out, fashion is funny) and has written on nearly every beat at daily newspapers in Colorado for more than a decade. She also writes a fitness column and has been a newspaper and magazine editor. She has a lengthy background of awards and honors, including eight first place awards, both state- and nationwide. She was named the top journalism graduate in the nation in 2001 and now is honored to be part of MediaNews Groups' Idealab, an elite group of twenty-five journalists nationwide tasked to shape the future of the field. Heckel has also edited and ghostwritten seven books; she runs multiple blogs; she is a social network guru for multiple companies; and she sells her soul in the form of words in any way possible—basically, if words are involved, so is she. Oh, and she loves poodles and lipstick. Stalk her at aimeeheckel.blogspot.com, where you can find links to all of the crazy projects she does.

Party of None

by Bob Woodiwiss

Two phrases are capable of making my right eyelid flutter with the erratic intensity of the wing of a chicken whose neck is being wrung. The first: "I need to check your prostate." (Which, I have to say; I find no less disturbing from medical professionals than from laypersons.) The second: "Let's have a party." In fact, this second phrase, most recently uttered by The Partner, so disturbs me I usually try to deflect it with, "How 'bout you examine my prostate instead?"

Party: Derived from the German, *"partiereicherdammerungen-hertz,"* meaning, "Feel free to treat my house with the disregard you usually reserve for a rental car." – *The American Heritage Dictionary, Fourth edition.*

As someone whose self-esteem is woefully dependent on the opinions of others, I find parties to be the ultimate in anxiety. There are simply too many opportunities to fail, fall short, disappoint. Will a lot of fun people show up or just the losers we know? Are brie Doritos too pretentious? Is one keg of beer enough, or will the guests want some, too? Are books-on-tape too conceptual to dance to? Thankfully, The Partner has the answers to all my questions. "Re-fucking-lax, anal boy," she suggests.

If your party is going to succeed, *every* detail is an *important* detail. For example, only after all the shriveled-up rich assholes you invited have RSVPed will you know *exactly* how many gold-digging whores you'll need to have in attendance. – Martha Stewart

We send out our invitations, some little dealees we designed on the computer. The 3-D font and insipid clip art give it a look that tells invitees, "They designed this little dealee on the computer." Messagewise, our invitation states the party's theme as, "The Fete of a Nation." That was The Partner's clever concept. Personally, I thought if the party had to have a theme, it should be something like, "Swingin' Celebration For People Who Promise They Won't Feed Our Dog Crab Dip or Hot Wings or Brownies or Other Crap But If They Can't Help Themselves and Break That Promise They Swear On Their Mother's Eyes They'll Come Back Tomorrow and Clean Up the Puke." The Dog, to my amazement, broke the tie in The Partner's favor.

Your house should be in perfect order before your first guests arrive. Not so much for their benefit but because it makes it so much easier to assess the total damage after they leave. – *The State Farm Insurance GoodTime Party Planning Handbook*

The invitation gives a start time of eight thirty. Predictably, the first arrivals don't show until nine thirty. And the bulk of the crowd – about fifty people – doesn't turn up until ten thirty, meaning this train may not run out of steam until the wee hours. I hold out until midnight and then start trying to drum up interest in my Nyquil Jell-O Shots. By one in the morning, feeling desperate and cruel, I pull out all the stops and start explaining Joe Lieberman's position on the Middle East.

Fish and Visitors stink after about three seconds when Ye are jamm'd into a room full of them. – *Benjamin Franklin*

While I'm timid, awkward, and a social tumor on occasions like this, The Partner is anything but. She is any party's vibrant, bright, warm, magnetic, engaging, easygoing, footloose, and energetic epicenter. She is JFK to my RMN. C3PO to my Hal. Pre-12/18/97 Chris Farley to my post-12/18/97 Chris Farley. Flipper to my fish sticks. I watch her mingle and dance and connect and before long I find myself wishing I had just 1 percent of what she's got. (I currently have 5 percent.)

Some people are made to circulate. Others to clot and cause strokes. – The Partner

It's 2:40 a.m. and the festivities are still in full swing. The food is holding, the beverages, ditto. A few couples sway Nyquilish-ly to Michael Crichton's *Airframe* (unabridged). Several guest-clusters have formed, talking, laughing, roaring, discussing every topic under the sun from the last good movie they saw to the last good movie they heard about. Me, I move invisibly through the tableau, emptying ashtrays, picking up abandoned paper plates, balled-up napkins, and exhausted drinks, avoiding eye contact, silently encouraging the group on the deck pummeling the guy who'd started playing his guitar. I briefly consider going to bed but find I'm in too much fear of the nightmare version of the bad dream I'm living.

Don't let your hosting responsibilities keep you from enjoying your own party. And don't let the fact that you spend all day, every day in your pajamas hinder your career advancement, either. – *Hugh Hefner's Guide to Life*

Dawn threatens; the last handful of guests exits, stepping out into the damp air. "You do a great party, man," someone says. Oy, that's just what I need; now I'll be up till noon trying to decide if he said that ironically or if I just heard it that way.

In Which I Get a Massage

by Mike Ball

Not too long ago I got my first real massage.

OK guys, go ahead and get all the stupid "Happy Ending" jokes out of your system. I'll wait. Finished? Good.

It just so happens that for my massage I went to a licensed massage therapist, a trained and highly skilled professional who had spent years studying and perfecting her craft. She was also a practicing nurse.

OK guys, get all the stupid "Naughty Nurse" jokes out of your system. I'll wait. Finished? Good.

The place where I booked my massage was called "Cosmic Hands…"

Really? OK, yeah, I'll wait.

As the day of my appointment approached, I have to admit that I became kind of apprehensive. After all, my previous experience with massage was limited, and not all that great.

Back in my youth, I played a little football (I was on the team as a voluntary tackling dummy). The team employed a massage therapist whose name, I'm pretty sure, was Thor. I didn't get to see him much, since he generally worked on the more productive players—the guys who scored lots of touchdowns, the other guys who were assigned to kill and eat opposing linemen, and the constantly injured linebacker who dated the head coach's daughter, "Crusher" (I'm guessing that this may not have actually been her real name).

The most memorable time I spent on Thor's massage table was when the big guy tried to cure a charley horse by taking my left foot and shoving the baby toe into my right ear.

During the years I spent as a competitive water skier, one of my coaches insisted that I undergo a form of massage called "Rolfing," which involved a very large woman with bionic thumbs, cast iron elbows, and a single eye in the middle of her forehead (that's the way I remember her) ripping out and rearranging all of my muscles while I shrieked and begged for either mercy or a quick death.

When I was playing Masters ice hockey (more often referred to as "Old Guys Who Skate Slow and Drink Beer in the Locker Room"), I spent quite a bit of time with the chiropractor having all my vertebrae systematically crushed and rearranged.

So when I walked through the door of Cosmic Hands I was mainly thinking that, in the interest of keeping up appearances, I should at least try to minimize the sobbing. As I stood there in the waiting room, though, I began to forget about my fear. The place was very appealing, tastefully decorated in a sixties retro kind of motif. The lights were soft, and the air was sweet with the scent of patchouli and incense. There was even one of those cool old hippie bead curtains leading back to the "business part" of the establishment.

Then, out through the bead curtains came the masseuse.

I had only spoken to her on the phone, and I was mildly curious to meet her face to face. What I had never considered was the possibility that she might turn out to be a neighbor. I didn't know the woman all that well, but I did run into her fairly frequently in the pet food aisle at the local supermarket. So when she led me into the treatment room, smiled, and said, "I'm going to step out for a few minutes while you get undressed," I wasn't sure exactly what to do.

To put this in perspective, I'm not particularly body shy. In fact, like most men I am downright delusional about my appearance.

As a short instructional aside for the ladies, guys develop and maintain our delusions by employing a number of meticulously crafted techniques. For instance, when it comes to mirrors, we never stand in front of one and critically "take inventory" like most women seem to do. We only look at ourselves from the shoulders up, and then only at certain carefully tested angles. That way we can wink at ourselves and say, "Looking good there, Stud," before we go off to try and find a belt that might still make it all the way around the equator and back to the buckle.

Many men also believe, despite all evidence to the contrary, that women are as anxious to feast their eyes our naughty bits as we are to get even the most fleeting glimpse of theirs. Luckily, I have been married for long enough to know *way* better than that. I understand that to most normal women, the sight of me in all my natural glory is more likely to be disturbing than thrilling.

What happened, as I stood there alone in that cozy little candlelit room, listening to the relaxing sounds of soft guitar music coming from the speakers near the head of the massage table, was that I decided that I would just strip down to my boxers. That way my friend could do her job and still be able to chat with me in Aisle Six without the specter of my "winky" hanging over her head.

Figuratively speaking.

Then I came to the realization, on that afternoon in the middle of July that, under my denim shorts (the ones with the manly rivets by the pockets and the macho tool loop on the side), I was wearing my "Curious George Christmas Fun" boxer shorts. I got a mental flash of how that might play out later in front of the Whisker Lickins. "Oh, hi," I would say. "What's new?"

"Nothing much," she would snicker. "So what did you get for Christmas from the Man in the Yellow Hat?"

So standing there next to the massage table, I had a decision to make. Do I 'fess up and just let her see the boxers? Do I abandon all modesty, strip down to nothing, hide George, and risk the whole winky-specter thing? Or do I stay fully dressed and wind up coming across like some deeply religious congressman on one of those occasional evenings when he is not out trolling for sex in an airport men's room?

I decided to stick with Curious George and hope for the best.

The masseuse was way cooler and more professional than I expected. She had a pretty good laugh, made a sort of call-back joke about Monkey Chow, and then said, "OK, Funny Guy, lose 'em. I've seen you walk, and I think we need to do a little work on loosening up your glutes."

If you don't know what "glutes" are, I'll wait while you take it to Google and then get all the stupid jokes out of your system. Finished? Good.

It turns out that the massage itself was really pleasant and deeply relaxing, with hardly any whimpering on my part. I can testify that by the time she was finished with me, my glutes were totally loose, and all my fretting about "Curious George Christmas Fun" was for nothing.

I'm just glad we didn't have to deal with the muscular guy in a loin cloth pictures on the "He-Man, Masters of the Universe" boxers I was originally going to wear...

QUICKIE from DC:

I love massages, and I love vacations. And prior to menopause, I coveted sex more than a Jersey Shore whore. Once, while I was on a (premenopause) vacation in Cancun and receiving a beach-front massage from a gorgeous man named Antonio, it began to rain. We moved to the vacant amphitheater of the resort. My friend Karen went to the bar to wait for me. Two hours later, she probably would have been pissed off if it hadn't been for the two-for-one Corona special. The massage was supposed to have lasted an hour, but Antonio was generous with his time, and I was grateful for the moregasm. We met again for more later.

__Mike Ball is__ an award-winning humorist who writes the internationally popular weekly syndicated column "What I've Learned So Far..." He lives and writes on the shores of Whitmore Lake, Michigan, sharing a roof with his wife and a psychotic Siamese cat. He is a member of the National Society of Newspaper Columnists, the recipient of the 2003 Erma Bombeck Award, and a finalist for the 2011 Robert Benchley Award.

Mike's first book, Bikes, Docks & Slush Nuggets, is Part I of the What I've Learned... So Far trilogy. Part II, Angels, Chimps & Tater Mitts, was released in April 2012. Part III, Banjos, Boats & Butt Dialing is "coming soon."

Mike is also a musician. As front man for the band Dr. Mike & The Sea Monkeys, he plays numerous instruments. The band features songs based on Mike's columns and books, such as, "At Least I've Got Most of My Hair," "Carlson the Pissed Off Angel," and "The Colonoscopy Song."

Mike is also the founder of Lost Voices, a Michigan nonprofit group that takes therapeutic roots music writing and performing programs to incarcerated and at-risk youth. For this work he was awarded the Kindness Community Hero Award from USA Today.

Is The King Your "Pop"?

by Nicole Knepper

My son was born old. Zach has always seemed beyond his years in the way he speaks and interacts with others. At three he could speak as clearly as most adults. He always regurgitated random facts of some sort and made sure I remembered to buy milk and lock the front door when leaving the house. I always felt like he was raising me, teaching me, guiding me through life.

Our friends, our family, and everyone else who came in contact with Zach would agree that my serious and thoughtful little boy was indeed unique. If you wanted to get a laugh out of him you had to earn it. At not quite three years old, he informed me that *if* my mom decided to remarry after the death of my father, I would just get another dad called a "step-dad" and he would get a new grandpa. I realize that empathy and understanding were sorely lacking when he made this statement; however, conceptually, my kid has always had a shocking level of comprehension and memory utilization. Thus, we dubbed him, "The Professor."

Now as fantastic as this was in terms of his remembering to turn off the lights when he left a room or putting his little

Underoos in the hamper, it was equally annoying when his steel-trap mind would consistently be able to sense the usual parental bullshit used for centuries to confuse and control young children. Santa Claus? That shit was debunked by Sherlock Zach while he was in kindergarten.

One hurried evening when Zach was seven years old, his random chitchat after his karate class was about babies. His little sister, Cate, had just started to toddle like a drunken monkey and was making a career out of being a menace, so I was chasing her through the parking lot. Zach asked me, "Mom, I know that the baby comes out of your vagina but how did the baby get *in* your vagina?"

My jaw karate–chopped the concrete. Really? Was he asking me this in the middle of the parking lot, all dressed up like a little kung fu dude, sporting all but one of his baby teeth? Indeed he was, and as I choked on air I decided that I would attempt to answer his question in the most roundabout way possible without going into the down and dirty details of the deed. Being ever so gently buzzed would have made this easier.

When I was pregnant with Cate, I gave Zach the little spiel about how the man's sperm combines with the woman's egg in order to create the baby. That happened after some brat at his daycare spilled the beans about the mommy/daddy collaboration. I repeated the sperm plus egg equals baby equation hoping it would suffice. A brief silence was followed by the inevitable question of *how* this process actually occurred.

"Does the man just let her eat it or what? Does she stick it *up* her vagina?" He asked this just as if he were asking for a snack. Although I'm sure some gold digger has done just that hoping for an eighteen-year payout from an NBA star, I couldn't justify appeasing him with that lie.

Calm and cool on the outside, my insides were aching for my little man to stay innocent. I'd take the incessant ramblings of a preschool-aged cherub obsessed with Spiderman any day over the questions of a preternaturally smart little man. Every inch of my heart and soul screamed, "Lie to him! Now's the time for that imagination of yours to shine, Momma, and shine bright. LIE, LIE, LIE!" before I realized that I had the perfect escape! "Honey, this is a conversation for home and not while we are in transition here, OK?" Grasshopper agreed to hold his curiosity until later when we were home, fed, and settled in for the night.

If you don't believe in miracles, just look for the silver lining. Mine came just an hour after we arrived home from karate class, in the form of a raging high fever and a kid too sick to even sit up. I would have even embraced an up all-night puke fest to avoid talking about sex with my son.

I dodged a bullet there and was pretty stoked that I didn't have to (a) stall for an hour or two until my husband arrived home to give me some support or (b) lie to my son. Up until this point I had never lied to my son. Aside from the Santa Claus/ Easter Bunny nonsense he had figured out in kindergarten, he also later informed me that if I lied to him again he would never forgive me and I would likely burn in hell (Christian preschool brainwashing clearly working).

I smugly toasted my success with a cocktail. Who the hell wouldn't? It's not often we moms duck in time to avoid getting hit smack in the face with tough questions and although the evening's victor was the result of some bastard virus, I was all about the metaphorical confetti of lime squeezed over my Goose and soda.

I know I mentioned that he has a good memory, right? He is a full-on powerhouse with near perfect recall of any book, song, television show, conversation, etc. When his fever broke and he was on the mend, there was no mention of his previous query. I was feeling slicker than laxative-induced shit at this point, because I truly feel that seven is too early to know the details of how babies are conceived, yet too old to be walking around with some kind of ridiculous and far-fetched notion about storks or whatever fanciful, developmentally appropriate nonsense I could dream up for him.

My luck ran out during a donut run while I was shoving some fried fat and hot coffee in my <u>grill</u> while driving the minivan.

"Mom, here's the thing that confuses me, OK? How do people *not* know if Michael Jackson is the father of his kids? If I gave a girl my sperm, I would know it, right? I know he's dead and nobody can ask him, but doesn't the girl know whose sperm she was eating?"

An eerie and uncomfortable silence followed. It was quiet initially because I had choked on a cruller, and after a short gagging and coughing episode it grew silent enough for Horton to hear the Who from a mile away. My initial reaction of shock quickly turned into amusement and it took all of my self-control to hold in the roar of laughter.

My little Professor was straight-up giving me the laser beam stare and looking for an answer. *fuckityshit* was all I could think. "This is it, girl. It's either showtime or a bold-faced lie followed by a slow burn in hell."

"Stay calm," I told myself. "You got this." Thankfully, I was adequately caffeinated, so I had the focus of an assassin. My first move was to pretend that the rearview mirror needed adjusting. I grumbled and acted annoyed and occupied myself with an unnecessary lane change and the biggest donut I could find in the box. I would have grabbed another donut regardless, pretending not to care what type of fat I'd be hogging down if it bought me another minute. I willed my daughter to burst into her usual tears of frustration that always appeared during her confinement in the car, but no luck. (Kids have shitty timing.)

I knew I had a choice to make. Utilizing the minivan as my classroom, I could avoid eye contact, improving the odds that I wouldn't bust a gut having to think about some guy just handing his sperm over to his lady friend while saying, "Here's my sperm," watching her swallow it, and then feeling all smug about his baby-making skills. Is that how Zach imagined it? GAH! I hated the fact that my husband wasn't there because often the most hilarious "kid incidents" occur with no witnesses, and they lose much of their entertainment value in translation. I had to act fast—the boy was waiting. Though they'd given me almost three solid years to avoid it, the miracle-makers of the universe had finally seen fit to spring on me the inevitable, and inevitably anxiety–producing, topic of sex: the horizontal mambo, the big nasty, screwing, fucking, banging. I was popping my birds and bees cherry.

Things went quickly from donuts to holes. I reminded him that the baby was in the uterus, *not* the stomach; his basic knowledge that girls had three holes "down there" and that the one in the middle was where the baby came out made that part relatively simple. Next I explained that in no way was the uterus connected to any part of the digestive system so if a woman swallowed sperm…well, *you* know!

Now I'd reached the really hard part. A quick reminder about where sperm comes out was met with two things: silence, and then "oooooooHHHHHHH nooooooooo." I knew immediately that The Professor had understood, but I still had to finish explaining until I was sure he was getting the facts straight. After all, he had the baby drowning in digested donut and men handing out spermy snacks to their baby-wantin' lady friends.

His response was basically what I had imagined: "*That* is so gross. *So gross!*" accompanied by all the gagging and throat hacking noises one might expect from a too-smart-for-his-own-good little man, followed up with a "Can we stop talking about this now?" I looked in the rearview mirror and saw that his little face was scrunched up and he was rubbing his eyes with his fists as if trying to erase the horrifying visual I had provided.

The kid used to be a huge Michael Jackson fan. His iPod was (and still is) chock full of tunes by the Jackson 5 and all the MJ greats like *Thriller, Beat it, Bad,* and songs from his early days as a solo artist. To me there is no question that Michael Jackson was talented, but his personal life was a hot mess. Even before his death I found myself struggling to answer questions about him. I believe that the entire conversation about where babies come from could have been avoided for another year if the King of Pop hadn't had to go and die during a very slow news week.

I will never forget learning about the birds and the bees. I was mortified as I sat at the kitchen table while my dad drew a sperm and an egg on a napkin and my mom sat there straight-faced and looking very interested in what he was saying. I wanted to disappear. All this because I had found condom wrappers when I was helping my mom make their bed? I should have kept my big, fat blabbermouth shut. I would have accepted candy wrappers as an answer.

I started noticing sounds in the night and realized that my parents had a flip lock on their bedroom door. The evidence that my parents were doing the dirty, disgusting deed was everywhere. Even today I can't take myself seriously during the act; it's *too* hilarious. Sex is just funny: The sounds, the awkwardness, pretty much everything related to bodies flapping—it's all further proof that God has a wickedly hilarious sense of humor. Don't get me wrong, I like doing "it"; Nikki likey sexy. However, I do not like to even think about my kid knowing that about 30 feet from his sanctuary, his momma and daddy are...well, *you* know. And wrapping my mom brain around the idea that my firstborn will one day "beat it"? Pass the vodka.

Nicole Knepper, *aka "Queen of Cussin'" or "Total Fucking Idiot," writes a moronic mommy blog. She is known for her pithy rants and off-color humor as well as being the most highly educated* know-nothing *to earn a diploma. ever. Her book,* Moms Who Drink and Swear: How to Love the Little Bastards in Your Life, *is being published by Penguin Group (NAL) in May 2013, just in time for Mother's Day; buy it so she can buy high-quality weed for after she puts her kids to bed. Find her blog at* http://www.chicagonow.com/moms-who-drink-and-swear/ *or on* Facebook *(Moms Who Drink and Swear).*

Spirited Engagements

by Rick Rantamaki

This summer, my wife thought it would be romantic if we celebrated our tenth wedding anniversary in Charleston, SC, the same "haunted" town where, a mere eleven years earlier, we were engaged. My wife's a ghost aficionado—she reads books about ghosts, she watches ghost shows, and, naturally, she's got the standard-issue, ghost-channeling Ouija board. So whenever she reserves us a room at a bed-and-breakfast, she always requests one that's notoriously haunted. How they're haunted, though, is a matter of interpretation.

Set the Wayback Machine for 1995, just about the time when a couple of English doctors were on the verge of cloning sheep (strictly for platonic reasons, of course) and OJ began his cross-country search for the murderous greenkeeper. I was on a weekend getaway with my future wife at a B&B in Charleston's historic district called the Sword Gate Inn, a former antebellum school for girls. Obviously, a house built in the early nineteenth century is going to accumulate some history, but unbeknownst to us, we were about to stoke its lore.

We had the honeymoon suite (we weren't even engaged yet), a spacious room that occupied the majority of the top floor. Its turn of the century furnishings were the type you'd expect to see from behind a velvet rope. The bare hardwood floors were composed of unusually wide planks that ran the length of the house. The mattresses on the canopy bed were piled to a height that made me consider sleeping with a helmet; no point in risking further brain damage.

Late one evening, we returned to the inn and decided to amuse ourselves with a game of quarters. For those of you unfamiliar with the game, the rules are simple—you bounce a quarter into a glass and then select someone to take a drink, a moot point with only two players, but hey, we were young.

I attempted to find a suitable playing surface by bouncing a quarter off the desk...the nightstand...the coffee table...and the cedar chest, but they were all "dead" surfaces. As a last resort, I tried the floor. The quarter nearly bounced back into my hand. Perfect. So, we rearranged the area rugs, repositioned the cooler, dimmed the lights, and settled onto the floor to begin our little showdown.

Mind you, my history with quarters hasn't exactly been stellar. When I first learned how to play, I thought, "This is easy." So of course I was swiftly, and soundly, defeated by a girl. That's right, a girl. It's not that she was gifted in the dexterity department, or that she'd spent years training in some remote Tibetan village; rather, she utilized a laughably simple technique. She would hover her chin just above the table while pressing the edge of the quarter on the bridge of her nose. When she released the quarter, it rolled down her nose, bounced once on the table, and then dropped into the glass...every time. If quarters was an Olympic event, I'm certain she would've made America proud. Needless to say, I woke up on the floor.

As it turns out, my date is a natural at the game too. Lucky me. She proceeded to methodically bounce the quarter into the glass tumbler and I, of course, drank...again and again. Like Pavlov's dog, each time the glass rang out, I'd automatically reach for my drink. I believe the game ended after I couldn't figure out which quarter to pick up.

The following morning we attended breakfast with the rest of the guests in the main dining room (though the mere thought of eggs was enough to upset my stomach). As I refilled my glass of water for the third time, one of the couples asked if we heard any strange noises during the night. They described it as a "click-ching" kind of sound. My date and I exchanged glances as the couple repeated in unison, "click-ching." The other guests suddenly recalled hearing strange noises too and they chimed in, "click-ching, click-ching."

A sweet little old woman at the table noticed we weren't joining the chant and asked in a concerned tone, "Didn't you hear it too, sweetie?", and began chanting along with the rest of them, "click-ching, click-ching, click-ching."

Of course I heard it, and I didn't need complete strangers replaying the sounds of defeat, especially while I was nursing a raging headache. I glanced towards the living room fully expecting to see Rod Serling sternly addressing the audience, "Submitted for your approval, one Richard J. Rantamaki. A man condemned to compete in a drinking game he can never win."

Fortunately, the innkeeper interrupted and explained that the noises must have been of the ghost which haunts the top floor of the house.

"Yes," I thought, "and she'll kick your [butt] in a game of quarters too."

The innkeeper told us a story about a schoolmistress who failed to keep one of her students from eloping. Tormented by guilt, her spirit constantly stands guard over the house.

The guests were enthralled with the innkeeper's ghost story, but not my date. Judging by her satisfied smile I figured she was basking in victory. Here it comes, I thought, she's about to reveal the true source of the "haunting" noises and soon the room will be filled with incredulous laughter over my inept skills with a quarter. After all, as a serious ghost enthusiast, she must set the story straight.

Then she spoke, "Yeah, we heard the noises too," and she looked at me and nodded her head, "Didn't we?"

Rather than call me out, she opted to toss our experience into the haunted lore of the Sword Gate Inn. She was willing to play along with the innkeeper's story and let the guests draw their own conclusions. That's when I knew she was my kind of woman. I joined her and the chorus of other guests, "click-ching, click-ching, click-ching."

Our departing entry in the guestbook simply read, "Enjoyed the spirits."

When we got married a year later, the click-ching of the champagne glasses during the toasts reminded us of our spirited game of quarters.

Rantamaki, Rick (ran-ta'-macky [Finnish]) Contributor to the Atlanta Journal-Constitution. *Born circa 1966, Quotes: "My existence alone proves humor knows no bounds."; on the Cereal Theory of Relationships, "Some settling may occur."; on the Adopted Theory of Relativity, "Everywhere I go DAMN there I am."* **noun** *1: Ohio-born humorist who, after stumbling upon a forbidden map of the United States (revealing other states), became the first in his class to relocate to a warmer climate. 2: Bumbling father, photographer, trail runner, engineer, IT manager, writer, and commuter who enjoys going bumper to bumper with his fellow rush hour captives. 3: Amateur weather guesser.* **verb** *1: To prank. "We waited till nightfall before we rantamakied their yard with police tape." 2: To heal with divine powers. "His presence alone was enough to rantamaki the computer."* **verb transitive** *1: To botch an ideal relationship. "Wedding bells were in the air, until I rantamakied the plans with my adolescent behavior."* **syn**: *see OAF, IDIOT, DOLT, FOOL, BAD DATE.*

Rick's a member of SouthernHumorists.com *(despite his Yankee heritage) and the* **CIA** *(Certifiable Idiots of America).*

She Golfs

by Shannon McKinnon

I would hate to run a golf course. Golfers have to be the most demanding people, always whining about something.

"The greens are too fast."

"The fairway's too rough."

"A bear ate Stanley."

People say they golf to relax, but that's a bunch of crap. I have golfed for years, and I have yet to see a relaxed golfer. The only relaxed golfer is the one teeing off at the first hole for the very first time in his or her life. This is a truly relaxed golfer.

Look at how cheerful she is. How happy.

She's swinging her club and laughing; clearly, she thinks she's here to have fun. She actually believes she's about to go on a leisurely stroll around a beautiful course with her husband, followed by a cold cooler and warm conversation at the nineteenth hole.

Stupid woman.

Neophyte.

She doesn't know that this game is to be taken seriously, that there is nothing leisurely about it. But fear not. There are lots of people around who will be more than happy to enlighten her. Like her spouse, who tells her that it doesn't matter if she swung at the ball twenty-three times and spent sixteen minutes searching for it in the woods just to get to the green. Never mind that she has finally reached the best part only to discover that someone else has beat her to it and planted a flag to prove it; she still must forgo hearing the satisfying plop of the ball as it drops into the hole on her very first green—she has spent far too much time on the hole already, and the course is backing up like a sewer.

"Pick up! Pick up!" says the spouse, his left eye twitching crazily. "Pick up the ball and let's go. Hurry!"

Golfing, the woman quickly learns, is not unlike participating in a robbery. You're not there to dillydally; you need to get in and get out, and the less evidence left behind the better. If a piece of grass is disturbed by your club, you must take the time to remove a metal pick from your bag and carefully prod it back into the earth. If you or your ball land in the sand trap, you must carefully rake over your tracks. If you lose your ball in the woods, search for it. However, be sure to wear a glove, so you don't leave any fingerprints behind. The rest of the time, though, thou shalt hurry. Thou shalt hurry hard.

"Is there something you want to tell me?" she asks her spouse as she jogs after him down the fairway, watching in alarm as he casts harried glances over his shoulder. "Have you got yourself involved with the…with the…the Mob?"

"What are you talking about?"

"Loan sharks? Drug dealers? Oh my God! I know exactly what it is. I know who's back there. It's your cousin Beth isn't it? She wants us to baby sit little Joey again, doesn't she? Come on man, shake a leg. We can run faster than this. Leave the clubs! Leave the clubs! I said, *abandon the clubs*!"

"Have you lost your mind, woman? Put on a hat, you must be getting sunstroke."

"Then why are we running?"

"We aren't running. We are merely picking up the pace. And by the way, course rules dictate that no one is allowed to hit the ball more than ten times per hole."

"But that's stupid. If I can only hit the ball ten times per hole, then I already know what my score will be."

After a few more times out, she starts to get the hang of it. She replaces her silly grin with a concentrated furrowing of the brow as she steps into the tee box. She hits the ball farther and walks faster. She learns to swear when the ball rolls into the sand trap instead of giggling foolishly. She even learns the art of raising her club above her head and bringing it down on the fairway with a soft thump to indicate displeasure when her ball ricochets off a spruce tree and plops into the lake.

She doesn't laugh anymore.

She golfs.

Shannon McKinnon's weekly column "Slice of Life" has been appearing in Canadian newspapers since 1991. Her humor-filled garden columns are a regular feature in Gardens West, Gardens Central, *and* Gardens East *magazines. She was the writer and editor at large for the 2012 edition of* Container Gardens, *put out by Harris Publications in New York.*

Shannon lives on sixty acres northwest of Dawson Creek, British Columbia in Canada (mile zero of the Alaska Highway). When she isn't writing, she is busy doing the organic thing and trying to live as simply and self-sufficiently as possible. She is married to her high school sweetheart, Darcy, and they have two grown sons. Sometimes she golfs. And sometimes she even enjoys it. You are warmly invited to follow her humor column at www.shannonmckinnon.com

SaunaFest

by Jamie Kiffel-Alcheh

"Sign this, please," a bouncer said as he thrust a piece of paper into my hand. 'It's strictly for publicity purposes."
I paused.
"I thought you said, 'stripping for publicity purposes,'" I said.
"No," he corrected, "but there will be filming."
It was 8:10 p.m. on an unusually warm fall night in New York City, and I was about to be admitted to SaunaFest. This was a Finnish invention involving an oversize sauna on the roof of the wildly avant-garde Gershwin Hotel, along with a DJ, and a performance of a classical Finnish play. All inside a sauna. Each $20 ticket came with two free vodkas.

In a fit of daring, I'd convinced three friends to join me: Evee, a slightly shy redhead who was studying to become a guidance counselor; Jie, a petite world-traveling anesthesiologist with the personality of a martial artist; and Jie's friend Oscar, a handsome, young Filipino doctor. None of us had any idea what to expect. The first question was obviously, Would we be dressed?

"I'm sure they'll give us robes or something," I speculated. "I mean, maybe it's not like a real sauna. Maybe you sit there in your clothes." The ad hadn't revealed any details.

I scanned the line behind us: Corduroy, casual jackets, turtlenecks. Then my gaze fell upon an older, well-dressed, stern-faced couple at the head of the line. They looked like Upper West Siders, once attractive and now preserved.

Swingers was the uncomfortable word that pronounced itself in my mind. I looked away.

We anxiously looked at our watches: eight fifteen. "What if we're late?" I whispered to my group.

"Excuse me," Oscar merrily asked the bouncer. "Are we going to make the eight o'clock seating?"

The bouncer made a funny face. "You'll be fine; people are just getting up there," he said.

Getting up? I wondered. I imagined Finnish people crawling out of sleeping bags.

Then the bouncer smirked. "Oh, you'll be very satisfied, I'm sure. Seems just about everyone is."

My friends and I shot uneasy smiles at each other.

"Hey, some guys dropped their drawers in there!" Jie piped up, pointing beyond the glass door.

"Where?"

"Come on in," the bouncer said, hustling us through. Somehow, the naked men disappeared as we were led to a small table just inside the door. A girl took our money and handed us each a wristband, a garbage bag, and a tiny towel. Then Jie, Evee, and I were pointed toward a closet-like room with no windows.

We all glanced at each other, trying not to show shock as we parted ways with Oscar and went inside our changing closet, a windowless room where a couple of girls were trying to force towels to cover both their upper and lower halves at once. "It's not a towel," one girl said flatly, holding up the scrap of material that, when wrapped, only covered the bottom portion of the breast and the upper portion of the rear. "It's a bathmat."

My own bottom made the so-called towel pop up in the back so that my psychedelic-printed bikini peeked out. Boy, I was thankful for that bikini. In concern for Jie, who had not been a Girl Scout and was not ever-prepared for rain, snow, or nuclear fallout, I gave her my tank top to wear. Evee was equipped with a camisole.

After reluctantly tossing our clothing into the trash bags we'd nervously left behind, we emerged.

Confused and mostly nude, we stumbled around the art-filled (and cold-floored) Gershwin lobby, which was empty except for a few unsuspecting patrons trying to check in (fully clothed). The hotel's front face, incidentally, is covered in modernist sculptures that are lit from within and resemble elephants' tusks. Inside, the walls are strewn with paintings and fabric hangings. It is ultra-chic and probably very expensive. But I didn't take in much of this because I was busy wondering if I was going to get arrested or put on *Candid Camera*.

After we spent a lot of time trying and failing to blend in with the scenery, a fully dressed guard pointed us to the elevators. We hustled inside the old, dark, tiny elevator, body to body with other nudists. Well, towel-ists. I noted that the guy in front of me had quite the athletic chest.

The doors heaved open and we stepped out into a narrow hallway.

Again, we looked around at the uninhibited inhabitants. A few people were already there, walking about in towels. They looked buff, albeit somewhat bewildered. I saw a lot of bare-chested men, most with stunning bodies. Then I stepped back as one man who weighed about three hundred pounds walked by clutching his towel at the side; it didn't go all the way around, and he was not wearing a bathing suit or underwear. Well, this was reality, after all. I just prayed that I wouldn't see a set of elephant-sized testicles swinging from beneath his Sumo-wrestler-sized butt.

"Where do we go?" Jie asked.

"Does anyone know where the sauna is?" someone else asked.

"Hey, guys!" Oscar emerged from a tiny room off the hall-way, wearing only a towel, a bare chest, and a big smile. He was carrying and a plate of hors d'oeuvres. "Get yourself a drink!" He looked like an Asian Hugh Hefner.

We lined up for the drinks. I ordered a screwdriver, figuring might really need it. That, or a pile driver and a good escape plan.

Sipping away, I observed the artwork that lined the walls: a woman exposing one breast, some nondescript shots, and, off the hallway, a small room where a Claymation movie was being shown. We ventured out onto the rooftop. Astroturf, a few tables, a tent, and something like a tiki bar were set up. A stout, wild-eyed, fifty-something Finnish man was DJing from behind the tiki extravaganza, interrupting the songs with what I thought was Finnish but later realized was broken English. He was doing some form of imitation-Michael Jackson arm dance. I believe he was missing a few teeth.

"Don't look at him," Evee hissed. "You'll encourage him."

I looked: he had a pendulum swinging from the edge of the bar, and he was waving his hand back and forth to make it move on the air currents. And he was grinning maniacally.

"Don't look!" she hissed again.

Obeying, I smiled at a thin, long-haired shirtless guy with a pierced septum and yin-yang lizards tattooed on his back.

"You go for those androgynous guys, don't you?" Jie piped, catching me looking.

"Should I introduce you?" Oscar asked excitedly. "Come on! Let me introduce you guys! Who is he? Where is he?"

Thankfully, at that moment Jie and Evee pulled me away toward the white tent. The sauna tent. A young Finnish guy wearing a turban and a Turkish towel drew back the flap with a flourish, and we were faced with approximately 12 square feet of dim, thick heat and wooden benches four levels high. The Finnish dude poured water on the coals, and the whole place steamed up.

"Oh, yeah," we all smiled, climbing onto the top bench and sidling in between sweating bodies.

Then, as my eyes adjusted to the dimness, I realized that the guy above me was completely naked. The guy next to him wasn't. I wondered if he knew that.

My eyes adjusted further: another naked dude was sitting right across from me! Still, I couldn't see *it* while he was sitting. I couldn't help looking at his rippling abs and broad, firm pecs. Then he stood up to put some water on the coals, and I did see It. Well, what there was of it.

"Wow, I'm amazed he's not embarrassed to be naked. I've never seen one that small," I whispered to Evee. "My nephew's at birth was twice the size of his."

"Hon…" she said, flatly, "that isn't so small."

"It's not?"

"You must have been really lucky so far," she shook her head.

Really lucky, I thought. Like several inches lucky.

"Even flaccid? Are you kidding? I mean there's nothing to work with here unless we put the thing in a splint."

I left all this alone for the moment and considered the fact that no one was really hitting on anybody. Perhaps we all needed to see a little less in order to stay interested.

Suddenly, I was getting splashed. "Eww," Oscar piped up. We looked and someone was hitting someone else across the back with a bunch of leaves dipped in a bucket of water.

"Cool!" I exclaimed.

"Ugh, dirty sweat!" Oscar the doctor said, and Jie agreed. They went outside to cool off a bit.

We surreptitiously tested the Norse bouquet before joining them outside.

"So where's the play?" Jie asked.

"No idea," someone said.

And then came more skin. I was glad I'd had that drink.

We saw her when we exited the sauna and stood on the roof, in the bright artificial light.

She was blonde, she was about 40, and she was naked. NAY-KED. NEK-KID, with huge, flopping breasts. I noticed manicured pubic hair; she must have thought her pubes were a putting green at a Pebble Beach golf course.

And there she stood in all her glory. Among the bathing-suited, the toweled, even the fully dressed press people in wool hats for goodness' sake, she was just carrying on conversations. Every time she turned my way, I felt like her enormous nipples were offering their services to breast-feed. She was a wet nurse waiting to happen.

It was unnerving, yet freeing in a way. Kind of like *National Geographic*.

And then, as with any good party, I was approached by a jerk. He wore blue boxer-briefs and had a great body and a good-looking face. I was standing in the hallway minding my own business when he flicked a lock of hair out of my face. I looked up, and he gazed into my eyes for a solid thirty seconds, slack-jawed, like he was about to fall forward out cold. I wondered if I should step aside, so I did. "Do you want to go to a party with me?" he said drunkenly.

"No," I concluded.

The next I saw of him, he was running his hand down the butt of the cute guy with the lizard tattoo. "You have a hot body, dude," he said. "I mean, first-rate. You should, like, be in magazines." I later learned that he'd hit on Naked Wet Nurse, too.

"Which dude?" Oscar asked enthusiastically when I explained what had happened. "Do you like him? Do you want me to introduce you to him?" Jie stopped him in time.

There really is something to meeting people while nearly naked, I must say. You get a very honest, unadorned view of them.

By ten o'clock that night, our experience had ended, but Oscar did have the chance to introduce me to one very straitlaced, good-looking Finnish guy. He was about as interested in me as in if he'd been offered a Quaker Rice Cake.

That's all right. I realized then—as I looked at him and recognized him from inside the sauna—that I could do better. I mean a good few inches better.

Jamie Kiffel-Alcheh's fiction has been widely published online and offline. She graduated magna cum laude from Wellesley College, where she received the school's highest honor for writing, the Mary Lyons '35 Prize. Her nonfiction work has won a Silver Clarion Award for Excellence in Journalism. She has served as editor in chief of "Vital Juice," the daily e-mail newsletter about healthy living, and as features and entertainment editor for Woman's World Magazine, *and she is a frequent contributor to* National Geographic Kids. *She is currently completing a novel.*

Peekers, Peckers, and Pervs

by DC Stanfa

I was jogging on a Florida beach when I plodded past a trouser trout. The offending creature belonged to a creepy old guy who apparently enjoyed pulling his shorts to the side as he passed unsuspecting girls and women, exposing himself during his lovely stroll down the beach. I was in my midforties and all too familiar with such crafty pervs, so I wasn't the least bit afraid. In fact, you could say I felt a bit cocky as I circled him twice (summoning my best Cagney and Lacey voice) and shouted, "Keep it in your pants, or you are going *downtown*!" I think I scared the pants back on him, as he and his snake shamefully slid away.

My fiancé, being a retired police chief, told me that there was a fine line between what I did and the illegal act of impersonating a police officer. Since I didn't actually claim to be a cop, he said I was probably within the letter of the law. I pointed out that the real crime was him impersonating a fiancé since he'd never officially asked me to marry him.

Say what you will about prolific Internet porn, I am just grateful that more of today's pervs can spank their monkeys in the pervacy of their own homes without going out looking for external stimuli like unsuspecting grade-schoolers.

Growing up in the sixties, boys were lucky to discover *Playboys* under their parents' beds. Now, they can innocently be looking for Dick's Sporting Goods online and get an unsolicited 3-D XXX sex ed lesson right in the middle of their mom's living room. Just ask my eleven-year-old nephew and his friends. Being the good boy that he is, my nephew immediately alerted his mom about the unwanted websites that were literally popping up like Whac-A-Moles, and my sister had to call his friends' parents and explain. But access to such explicit content really raises the bar for your average sixties and seventies window-peeker.

While living in our small, one-story house on Indianola, in Toledo, Ohio, we had three window-peekers — that we know of, anyway. My two sisters and I were so close in age that we could pass as triplets, or at least Catholic triplets. We were the Midwest version of the Brady girls. Lori was the popular but pushy Marsha. I was awkward Jan (complete with imaginary boyfriends). Sherry was Cindy—she even had her own darling speech impediment for a while. Mom, "Glo"-sounds-like–"Flo" as in Florence Henderson, even had the same cute blond shag as Mrs. Brady. I'm sure if the Bradys hadn't been richer than we were—able to afford a two-story home custom-designed by Mr. Brady himself—they would have had their own window-peekers as well.

In retrospect, the Stanfas should have converted from curtains to blinds after Chucky Pedephilo, our eighteen-year-old neighbor, tried to catch a glimpse of our prepubescent private parts and was tackled outside our window by my pajama-clad dad, Denny, atop a snow drift in 1969. The second peeker was only witnessed by me, as I dressed for school in sixth grade. The curtains were 95 percent closed, but I could see an eyeball and part of a nose in the 5 percent crack. I ran out of the room screaming. He didn't hang around to meet the cops (or worse, my dad), and was never identified. I still have nightmares where I look out the window and see someone staring back.

The last Indianola window-watcher appeared well after all the Stanfa girls had reached puberty, making it slightly less disturbing if you choose to rank these kinds of events but still plenty creepy. This time, our neighbor got the license plate number of the offending car. My dad might have gotten the tag number anyway since he'd slammed a wooden mop into the trunk of Peepy the Perpetrator's car as it sped away.

At the time, my mom was serendipitously working in the security department at the university. Her coworker ran the license number to get the perv's name and address, even though he wasn't supposed to. We'd also reported the incident to the Toledo Police Department. My dad borrowed a shotgun from a coworker and stashed it in the living room next to the La-Z-Boy.

While the TPD investigated, Glo and Denny drove past the address they'd tracked down. They recognized the car in the driveway, mop-dented trunk and all. They tipped off the police, and finally Perv was arrested. He entered a plea bargain for a lesser charge of trespassing. We were all disappointed that he'd "gotten off" because apparently he'd had other sexual offenses, including breaking and entering—and attempted rape. He'd also been convicted of another B&E in which he'd "gotten off" in that woman's undergarments. Denny kept that shotgun for a long, long time.

Parks and Masturbation has been regulation recreation for pervs for as long as wankers have been wanking. For this fifth-grader, shortcutting through the park after swim lessons became a thing of the past after a man stepped out of the woods to cross her path with what looked like a kielbasa in his hand. I was traumatized, but luckily he didn't pluck me or my sister off of our bikes. We have often wondered if we wouldn't have been so lucky if we'd been riding through the park alone.

I wish I could say this was the extent of my stories of the attack of the unwanted schlongs, but who can forget The Bottom Half? Believe it or not, that was the actual name of a jeans store where I worked at the mall during high school. One day, several female customers reported a man flashing them from a unisex dressing room. He'd been in there quite a while with the door wide open. The store manager was on his lunch break. I walked back to check out the bottom half situation. Sure enough. He couldn't have been prouder unless he'd been a peacock or, perhaps a porn star. I called mall security and they took him away. My manager had to take care of the present the perv left on the mirror. He also told me that the guy was a repeat beater, as he'd already been arrested three times at this mall and was actually banned from it.

As an adult, I've witnessed several more weirdos whacking their mackerals, but have reacted differently each time, as each situation has been *unique*. After so many incidents, including my younger sister Sherry being followed home from grade school, I delved during college into the psychology of what makes these sick dicks tick. Voyeurs and exhibitionists have the same sexual motive: sexual gratification. Both behaviors can start out passively and continue to get more aggressive until they develop into more serious and sexually deviant criminal actions. Regarding the fond-of-fondling–themselves-while-flashing, part of their sexual arousal comes from enjoying their victim's reaction—which is usually fear. If that emotion continues to feed their fantasy, the crimes can escalate to physical attacks, including rape and murder. So, I vowed to never feed the cockroaches fear, ever again.

I began my glamorous career selling empty cardboard (corrugated, for us professionals) boxes, in the great state of Texas in the early eighties. Traveling to and fro, up and down interstates and farm-to-market roads could be tedious or scenic. This was the era before cell phones, so my eyes were always on the road. While driving from Dallas to Waco, I encountered an erratic driver in a tiny truck who was playing cat and mouse—I was the mouse, and he was trying to trap me. When I sped up, he was right next to me. If I slowed down, he did, too. I had a sick feeling and instinctively knew what he was doing. I decided to show him that he was "barking up the wrong tree," a euphemism for masturbation, which I discovered on the website *dribbleglass.com/subpages/euphemisms* along with more than two hundred other useful phrases including such gems as "fly fishing" and "exercising your right."

I had exercised my right to not give the driver the satisfaction he was looking for, which at minimum was to look at him. But I had to end this game somehow, and it was not going to be a win/win. I slowed down to about thirty miles per hour, and as he pulled up next to me, I could see him in my periphery "brushing up on his typing skills." I held my breath, looked him straight in the one-eyed lizard and pronounced it "tiny," while shaking my head in disappointment and giving him a measurement with my thumb and forefinger. After I gave him an inch, I gave myself a mile—at about a hundred miles per hour—to the downtown exit, where I easily located the Waxahachie Police Department. I reported the incident and gave them the license plate, the vehicle, and a description of the Waxahachie Wacker.

They ran the license number and the officer proclaimed, "Well, that there's Bobby Kitchens. Yeah, we know him. Boy's been in plenty a trouble. 'Course his momma's in prison for shooting his daddy dead."

I felt like I was in a movie, because the southern cop was so cliché and so matter of fact, almost droll, as he spilled the back story.

"Bobby's been in prison hisself for several sexual offenses, and there's an outstanding warrant for him in Dallas, a rape charge. We just cain't seem to catch up with 'im."

I occasionally checked in with the WPD to see if they had gotten a bead on Bobby and was always told they "still cain't find 'em."

# # #

My best friend Karen is the perfect traveling companion. She is completely content in any situation as long as there is a cocktail at hand. She never gets frazzled over things like cancelled flights or lost luggage; they're just good reasons to have more cocktails. And besides, she often says, "Someday you'll write a really funny story about this."

Karen never wants to go do the usual touristy things like narrated tours of historic areas. And you won't catch her shopping at a straw market—ever. Our usual beach vacation plans were simple: Be poolside with cervezas with limes. No need to get any more ambitious than that. However, on an Acapulco adventure in the late nineties, we made an exception and made actual plans— to attend a Mexican version of the Chippendales show. Lured by the $10.99 all-you-can-drink Coronas and no cover charge before seven p.m., we arrived early and were soon happily into happy hour; the show started around nine. The first two guys remained almost fully clothed, and we couldn't hide our disappointment. But the pace picked up pretty quickly after that, and soon there was a stage full of buff men gyrating around in G-strings, for which we were grateful.

One particularly lithe Latino ripped off his schlong thong and left the stage, reappearing at the bar and in the audience; he held something in his hand. As he approached me, holding it out, I thought it was some kind of joke he was playing; it looked like a big chorizo. He took my hand and placed it on the sensational sausage, and I quickly pulled it away when I realized it was a *real, erect penis.*

I'd felt a few of those before.

As he sauntered over to another table, I exchanged oh-my-gods with Karen.

"Is there a sign on your forehead, DC? Show me your dick, let me hold it." She knew I'd certainly seen more than my share, both accidentally and on purpose.

There were a few men in the audience with their wives or dates, and I wondered what they must have been wondering. Until Chippendick presented his package to a middle-aged woman—and SHE PUT IT IN HER MOUTH while her husband beamed with pride as if she'd just won the best apple pie contest at the county fair.

Soon after that, several dancers pulled some women onto the stage and dirty danced with them. They ended up lying down on top of them, performing simulated sex acts. We didn't wait around for our turn as we wondered out loud if there were going to be more blow jobs or a full blown orgy.

"When do you think they'll bring in the donkeys?" Karen asked as we bolted through the exit, laughing hysterically.

Congenial Karen got in the front seat of the taxi, wanting to chat with the driver, using the only three short phrases she knows in Spanish. Karen told me later that as we weaved our way through the mountains toward our resort, the morbidly obese cab driver kept putting his hand on her thigh and she kept flicking it off. She said she didn't know the Spanish word for *stop.*

Several years later in Cancún, we took an uncharacteristic trip to an underground river park which we regretted within the first ten minutes of the hour and a half after we discovered there was no bathroom on the bus. Upon arriving at the park, our raging hangovers gave way to exhaustion, and we attempted to nap in some hammocks. Karen dozed off immediately, but I couldn't sleep. Apparently, neither could a teenage boy about forty yards from me. Out of a half-closed eye, I spotted him congratulating his chorizo, with his eyes fixed on us. He pointed his erection in our direction. I shut my eyes tight and wondered about that sign on my forehead, concluding that it must be written in both English and Spanish and wondering how I could change it to a STOP sign. By the way, Karen, for future reference, that's HALTO in Spanish.

The Desperate Dad's Guide to Getting Some

By Jackie Papandrew

Modern moms, it seems, are just not in the mood. Pummeled by children and chores, exhausted by careers and car-pools, once-hot mammas are now too whupped for whoopee, too crabby to conjugate. I hate to say it, fellas, but at day's end, we'd often rather curl up in the baggiest pair of granny panties we can find and hit the hay without you.

Coincidentally, scientists have been *shocked* recently to discover that women are much more genetically complex than men. It turns out that the female's double X chromosomes operate on a far deeper molecular level, which explains why we are able to pick up our socks and throw out pizza boxes in a timely manner. Hmm…could *our* lack of libido and *your* genetic simplicity be somehow related?

So for all you befuddled bearers of the Y chromosome (aka *men*), I offer a short Do and Don't List that just might help you get some XXX action tonight:

DO the windows. And the dishes. Scrub the sink, clean the toilet. Formula 409 is foreplay, baby.

DON'T promote pain. Try not to suggest surfaces for sex that are likely to cause discomfort. This would include floors, where we are bound to be impaled by an errant toy, and walls, where we will feel like concrete on the wrong end of a jackhammer. Forget any grainy videos you may have seen of surgically enhanced women who appear to enjoy having sex under these conditions. They are being paid to fake it. We, on the other hand, are faking it for free, and we require a soft stage on which to perform.

DO take a cuddling class. Really. You have to do more than sling one heavy, hairy arm across our chests a microsecond before you begin snoring. Professional help is available.

DON'T blame the hormones. If we seem annoyed, assume it is your fault and strive mightily to mollify us. Do not automatically chalk it up to the vagaries of menstruation. Doing so will ensure long cycles of celibacy.

DO let us sleep in. Corral the kids and keep them quiet. Then bring us breakfast in bed. This will release passion-promoting endorphins all through our bodies that by nightfall will have us convinced you are Brad Pitt. We might even slip into that negligee you bought years ago, the one with the price tag still on it.

DON'T try to multitask. This is a feat best left to the women. We are designed to do many things at once. Your multitasking abilities are limited to flipping channels, drinking beer, and making love. Enacting all three simultaneously, however, will cause our hackles to rise and our interest in you to cool. Do not attempt to trick us by innocently suggesting a sexual position that facilitates your multitasking effort. Remember, we are the genetically superior species. We need your full attention, and we cannot be fooled.

DO get a room. Occasionally, sweep us away to a hotel, one with immaculately clean sheets, a hot tub the size of our kitchens, and soft terrycloth robes. Think Ritz Carlton here, not Motel 6.

DON'T follow formulas. My husband stubbornly clings to a belief that he has a ten-minute window of opportunity between the time I finish my wine and the time I am blissfully asleep. (I don't know where he got this idea.) He calculates every activity so that we are back in the bedroom within the required time frame. This severely limits our culinary opportunities and makes me grouchy as a grizzly. Do not try this at *your* home.

DO turn into a tool man. No, not that kind of tool, at least not yet. Cheerfully take on home improvement projects. A friend of ours built a laundry room for his wife in hopes of "getting some good sex out of it." This is a wise, and undoubtedly well satisfied, man.

DON'T make stupid comments. My husband was once foolish enough to point out, just after initiating a lovemaking session, that I seemed to be developing a beer belly. (I was *obviously* retaining water!) It's at times like this that I realize God has a wicked sense of humor. Unlike ebony and ivory, X and Y shouldn't even be on the same keyboard.

DO remove your socks. Leaving your socks on feels quick and dirty and will make us think we should post an hourly rate on the back of the door.

AND FINALLY...

DON'T threaten the children. If you are a victim of *coitus interruptus* caused by a wandering child and an unlocked door, avoid yelling at the youngster. Gracefully flip on your back, with no audible obscenities, and swiftly yank up the covers. And *don't* throw anything at the poor tot who wonders why Daddy brought his drill to bed.

Jackie Papandrew airs a lot of dirty laundry on her Facebook fan page (36,761 fans as of right this minute), which seems to amuse the deviant group of folks who frequent the page. She's the author of two humor books — Airing My Dirty Laundry *and* The Desperate Dad's Guide to Getting Some *— as well as a motley mix of lifestyle articles, parenting primers, and business writing. Her humor columns have appeared in newspapers such as* The Cleveland Plain Dealer, *The Tampa* Tribune, *and* The Oklahoman, *as well as in the* Chicken Soup for the Soul *books and many other publications. Jackie has won a Neal Award from American Business Media, as well as awards from the Oklahoma Press Association, Parenting Publications of America, America's Funniest Humor Press, and the Florida Freelance Writers Association.*

When she's not airing dirty laundry or advising desperate dads, Jackie cuts an imposing figure in the business world (or not) as the CEO of Bare Board Group, a supplier of printed circuit boards with offices in Florida, Canada, and Taiwan. Bare Board Group was recently included on the Inc. 5000 list of fastest-growing private companies in the United States.

Let's Talk About Sex

By Tracy Beckerman

I don't know too many parents who would tell their kids where babies come from before their kids actually ask, present company included. Ask me about religion, death, the existence of tooth fairies, I'm a regular encyclopedia of parental knowledge. But ask me about sex, and suddenly I clam up. Not that I don't know about it; I do have two kids, after all. But explaining it in technical terms to my kids—well that's about as high on my list of favorite activities as cleaning the toilet bowl.

Somehow, much to my relief, I made it to my children's sixth and eighth years without having to deal with that topic. And then one day as I was carpooling three second-graders and my six-year-old daughter home from school, my son announced that someone had said a bad word at recess that day.

"What's the word?" I asked him.

"S-E-X," he spelled. I jerked the car over to avoid hitting a tree.

"What's that spell?" asked my daughter.

"Sex! It spells sex!" yelled one of the other kids in the car. "And it's *horrible*."

"It's not horrible and it's not a bad word," I said, trying to maintain my composure lest I alert the kids that we were in dangerous parenting territory by accidentally running over someone's cat. I wondered why these things always came up when my husband was away on a business trip.

I took a deep, cleansing breath. "Does anyone know what it is?" I asked. The three older kids all said yes. That two of them knew didn't surprise me. One of them was something of a junior scientist and the other watched MTV. That my son knew, however, absolutely floored me. I knew I hadn't told him and his father hadn't told him, so unless they had started teaching that particular lesson on *Rugrats*, I didn't have a clue how he found out.

"What do you think it is?" I asked my son.

He explained it. Suffice it to say, he was mostly right…except for the part about something getting "stuck."

Aside from this minor correction, I was saved the trouble of having to delve into the actual nuts and bolts of sex. And I was more than happy to change the subject and ignore my daughter yelling from the backseat, "Wait, I don't understand. The man does what?" until my son said, "But why do people do that?"

"To make babies," said his friend, the junior scientist and designated human sexuality expert.

My son grimaced. "Is that the *only* way?" he asked with a shudder.

"No," said the expert. "They can mix parts of the man and woman in a dish and then when the cells join together, they put it in the mother to grow into a baby." I was impressed. But I imagined my son picturing a man's leg and a woman's elbow being stirred in a soup bowl.

"I think that's how I was made," announced my son.

I snorted. "Why do you think that?"

"Because you and dad wouldn't do that *other* thing," he said with certainty.

"*Surprise!*"

He suddenly looked exhausted, as though the weight of this knowledge was too much for his little eight-year-old mind to bear. Actually, it was almost too much for my thirty-eight-year-old mind to bear. Fortunately we had arrived at our destination, and I was able to suggest that we table the conversation for another time.

Later that night, after I put my daughter to bed, I sat my son down and explained about the birds and the bees, and why sex isn't so horrible when you're an adult and you love someone and want to have a baby.

I answered all his questions, and when he didn't have any more, I tucked him in and kissed him goodnight.

As I walked down the hall, relieved that this day was finally over, I heard my daughter call from her bedroom.

"Mommy, Mommy. Where do babies come from?"

I sighed. "The stork brings them."

"Is that after the storks have sex?"

Tracy Beckerman writes the humor column and blog LOST IN SUBURBIA®, *which is syndicated to over four hundred newspapers in twenty-five states and on two hundred fifty related websites to about ten million readers (give or take a thousand). She is the author of two books,* Rebel without a Minivan, *which is a compilation of her earlier columns, and* Lost in Suburbia: A Momoir. How I Got Pregnant, Lost Myself and Got My **Cool** Back in the New Jersey Suburbs, *will be published by Perigee books in early 2013.*

Tracy has appeared on The Today Show *on NBC,* The CBS Early Show, Better TV, LX NY, *and* CBS Sunday Morning with Charles Osgood, *among others, and does stand-up comedy about how to be a cool mom in the suburbs. Yes, she knows that is an oxymoron.*

She has won a Writer's Guild of America Award and a New York EMMY® for her writing, is a past recipient of the Erma Bombeck Humor Writers Award and a National Society of Newspaper Columnists award, and was selected as America's Top Blogger by The Balancing Act on Lifetime Television.

She speaks frequently at conferences about whatever comes to mind at the moment.

Neither Heads Nor Tails

by Liz Langley

Best American Travel Writing 2000 features the brilliant, bizarre, funny story "Winter Rules," by Steve Rushin of Sports Illustrated. It's a sidesplitting tale about ice golfing in Greenland. When talking about local cuisine, Rushin quotes some descriptive text about reindeer stomach: "It is neither delicious nor revolting, but somewhere in between."

That is how I would describe "The Puppetry of the Penis," a show which, like a patch of pansies growing out of a volcanic rock, has found itself flourishing in a place you'd never have thought it would. It seems like the kind of thing that should have stayed in the bathroom of a bored and very lonely man, or in the treasure chest of memories of two men who spent a drunken evening together that they will never tell their sweethearts about. Where it ended up is off-Broadway at the John Houseman Theater.

The title is self-explanatory: two men making shapes out of their genitals for an audience. The two young Aussies who started the show have left it, presumably for jobs that don't involve publicly swinging their wangs around like lassos. They were replaced by two new Aussies, Daniel Lewry and Jim MacGregor,

161

who make a grand entrance wearing nothing but long capes and sneakers, and within minutes lose the capes and are bending their schlongs like balloon-folders and making clever dick-related jokes while they're at it. The shapes they make out of their own genitals include the "snail," the "pelican," the "Eiffel Tower," and the "baby kangaroo," inside its mother's pouch.

Tough act to follow

Wait, you're squinting. Let me help. Here's a graphic description of how they made the Loch Ness monster, so you can really see it in your mind, as I'm sure you'll want to: Take testicles and move off to one side, creating the serpent's body. Take penis and make into an upside down J, facing the opposite way from the testicles, providing the monster's neck and head. Voila! Nessie! And as with Nessie, nobody fully believes what they're seeing. (If you don't have male genitals handy, substitute a couple of kiwi fruits and a sock.) The finished shapes were projected onto a giant screen behind the players, in case people in the back didn't get a good enough look. And, well, a penis the size of a couch is not as pretty as one might think, and one develops a great sense of empathy for Faye Wray and the eyeful she must have gotten on her first date with King Kong.

Having naked men cavorting around in front of you isn't as pretty as you might think, either. I felt much the way you do when you see a couple fighting or a dog pooping on the sidewalk: I shouldn't be witnessing this. Two other girls and I, sitting in a row, reacted with definite and identical body language: one crossed arm, one hand over the mouth, i.e., "Oh my God" and "Don't come near me."

I laughed the whole time. How can you not? When men are stand before you stretching their bathing-suit parts into shapes such as "baby bird," "hamburger," and "didgeridoo," you laugh because it's funny. It's also embarrassing and bizarre, and the mix makes laughter inevitable. The audience reacted appreciatively and included a boy about eleven years old and a man, sitting behind him, who looked blankly at the two performers with the "You'd better be kidding," expression of a father whose son just swore that the drugs in his car belonged to a friend.

Don't try this at home

I've heard "The Puppetry of the Penis" described as the male response to "The Vagina Monologues." I read the script of the latter, however, and at no point did I come across naked women showing how they can make a butterfly, a lily, or the Cingular Wireless logo.

Speaking of women, I wonder how many who have viewed this at some point, got drunk, and tried to make a muppet out of their partner's willie. The guys onstage make this Stretch Armstrong/Plastic Man activity look so easy, it seems almost silly not to try it on someone else. The physical pain would seem minor compared to the emotional trauma brought on by one's partner wanting to see "what it looks like as a pelican," and, of course, laughing right at it, which would probably lead to break-ups if not mental collapse. Also, I asked a man and found out that this is not something they all do, even in childhood. Most never think, "I wonder what it would look like as a greyhound," and put a champagne cork wire over it. Just these guys.

So, like the reindeer stomach (in which Rushin finds a metaphor for life), these penis puppets were neither delicious nor revolting. I laughed, but the anticipation of going was more thrilling than having gone. I didn't flee the room, but I didn't bring it up in conversation often thereafter. And the bottom line is that I can say whatever I want, but I'm the one who paid to see genital puppetry. So who's the real wiener?

Sleep Marry Syndrome

by Leigh Anne Jasheway-Bryant

You ou wouldn't think it'd be possible to be both a good girl and a tramp, but somehow I've managed. What can I say, I'm an overachiever.

Before getting into the heart of the matter, you should know that I have been married three times. Don't think of them as failed marriages—I don't. I think of them as "promotions." Almost no one wants to stay at the same job for more than a decade, so every ten years or so, I put out feelers, send out my resume, and buy new interview clothes. Although, now that I'm in my fifties, I'm thinking about retiring.

It's not the multiple marriages that qualify me as trampish. At least I get married; I've seen the statistics, and the rest of you are out there shacking up. Which I have no problem with, except that you can't register for wedding gifts at Target. Which is just a darned shame.

No, what makes me a hussy is that I slept with all of my husbands before we got married. Way before. Once before we'd been formally introduced. What can I say? I need to sample the merchandise before I'm ready to order the product. Really, it's not sex, it's market research. What did women do in those virtuous times when they knew they were getting a gravy boat, but had no idea what alien vessel was coming in south of the border? What if you married into something tragic, genitaliawise? If you unfurl the sails before you buy the veil, you find out what's gonna rock more than the just the gravy boat. It gives you the chance to negotiate the size of the dowry.

Before you go getting all judgmental, here comes the good girl part...Not only did I eventually get married, uh, thrice, but I eventually married every man I ever slept with. Which by my count is...three. How many of you can say that about your sexual trysts, hmmm? Those of you who've had sex with nine, twelve, forty-seven guys—imagine marrying them all! Unless you're Erica Kane on *All My Children*, who'd even have the time?

I think I have a psychological problem that hasn't yet been identified by the American Psychological Association. I refer to it as "SMS," or Sleep Marry Syndrome. Every time I and my fellow SMS sufferers sleep with someone, we end up saying "I do" to more than just "Do you like to be on top?" (By the way, why do we call it "sleeping with" anyway? It's either sleeping or having sex for the most part, and never the twain shall meet.)

They say that sex is a way we mammals bond to one another, especially we women. For most of the rest of the world, sex is like Velcro. For me, it's like Super Glue.

Take my current (and last, if you can believe my threats of retiring) husband. I met him the old-fashioned way...in a bar. Bars are great places for middle-aged people to meet because it's so dark you can't see each other's crows' feet and love handles. And I thought it was sexy the way the light from the disco ball bounced off his little bald spot.

Within minutes of meeting, I blurted out, "You need to know, I'm never getting married again." Yep, that's me, ever the sterling conversationalist. A look of relief washed over his face. He smiled and said, "That's refreshing. Most women your age are desperate to get married so they don't have to grow old alone." (Yes, he is also blessed with the ability to say the wrong thing at the right time.) We grinned at each other like chimps that had just groomed each other of ticks. "Oh," he added, "I should tell you that I never want to be in a long-term relationship again. I'm just not good at them."

A week later, as we lay sweaty on the floor in his apartment, having just made wild monkey sex for the first time, he proposed. Well, he proposed to propose. Something along the lines of, "I may just have to ask you to marry me one day." And I, firmly entrenched in my SMS, nodded my head and accepted.

Hmmm…now that I tell the story, maybe I'm not the only one with a problem. It's not like I've actually asked anyone to marry me. Nor have I stalked someone until they broke down and bought me a ring. That's something that might look like fun in the movies, but I tend to shy away from things involving restraining orders and police action until the divorce proceedings.

The truth is, it's the guys who fall for me after sex. My only sin is that I say yes when the question is popped. I could look at this whole situation as a huge compliment about just how good I am in bed (and I am good — I don't hog the covers, snore minimally, and only kick when I'm excited). Perhaps I exude some kind of pheromone that's released during sex and causes men to forget their fear of commitment, their pledges never to get involved or married, their belief that marriage is a rotten idea dreamed up by the producers at the Lifetime Network, etc., and throw their hats and the third fingers on their left hands in the ring. Maybe I should use a different deodorant.

I guess I'll never know whether SMS is psychological or chemical. But I think I've found a way to solve my problem should the situation ever arise in the future. The minute a man starts to talk to me, I'm going to respond with, "Every man I've ever had sex with, I've married." That should ensure that we never so much as fantasize about each other.

Problem solved! Goodbye tramp, hello good girl!

QUICKIE from DC:

My friend Anita swears she suffers from a disorder which renders all the men she's ever exchanged body fluids with certifiably insane. Her theory (and I am a witness to her defense) is that she is a "carrier" of some mind-grinding enzyme that is passed to her partner. Be it a French kiss or full-on fornication, perfectly upstanding gentlemen turn into where-are-you wolfs and various other stalker types. She's a walking lollipop lunatic factory.

She's still single, and looking for a cure. So, guys, no more body shots with strangers...

Leigh Anne Jasheway *won the Erma Bombeck Humor Writing prize in 2003 with her true column on how her first mammogram caught on fire. She's the author of eighteen books, including* Bedtime Stories for Dogs *and* Not Guilty by Reason of Menopause. *She writes a monthly humor column for the* Register-Guard's Dash *magazine and has written for dozens of magazines and 'zines. Leigh Anne is also a nationally known humorous motivational speaker and stress management expert, as well as a stand-up comic, comedy coach, editor, and grammar instructor. Her website is* accidentalcomic.com.

The Devil Juice Made Me Do It

by Susan Reinhardt

Dear Yancey County School Board, Yancey County Board of Commissioners, and any other party affiliated with my husband,

I know he is the attorney for your organizations and is quite upstanding unless he gets into the white liquor and starts dancing wildly and propositioning the cute Clerk of Court. This is why I have to confess my social media criminal activity.

I did hijack his Facebook page, but I had his permission. He was reading a crime novel and I asked, "Donny, do you mind if I use your Facebook page to start a blog about sex, drugs, and whatnot? You never go there, so I figured I could skip the traditional ways of blogging and just claim your home page."

"Sure," he said, not looking up from his book. I realize now that he wasn't really listening, (just like when I say, "Am I fat?" and he says, "Sure" and I get all pissy and refuse blowjobs for a week.)

So I'm apologizing for all the crazy stuff I wrote, you know about the Western Sizzlin' seafood buffet giving people gas and making bloated sex nearly impossible, or the man who released his foot-long tongue and licked the back of my aunt's neck as a unique way of saying hello.

All of this is really the fault of the company that makes Red Bull. You see, I drank one and it altered my state of mind. I think it would be a good idea to ban Red Bull in Yancey County, and all other counties for that matter.

Please don't fire Donny if you saw my blog on his page. I have taken it down, due to one reader objecting and accusing me of identity theft and other things that could mean doing time. She had the nerve to accuse me of being nasty just because I mentioned something about men with small penises compensating with their cars, wallets, and Louis Vuitton luggage.

Needless to say (except actually quite necessary to say), while I was blogging, everything was going really kick ass wonderfully. His friends (and I confirmed all three hundred friend requests since he doesn't use his page) seemed entertained with my offering, which simply fueled the fire.

Red Bull will do that. It says it right on the can: It increases performance and makes you feel more energetic, thus improving your overall well-being. It can lead to rapid-onset mania, which is a nice word for a mental illness only such meds as Depakote* will cure. See the end of this story, if you even read that far, to find out what Depakote is, OK?

What a giant can of Red Bull actually does is make you more hyper than a crack-addicted squirrel (Yes, rodents do get hooked on street drugs), and things come out of your head and right onto social media sites like Facebook.

Red Bull is like meth. Well, I've never tried meth, but I'd bet it's a first cousin or even a brother to energy drinks. Anyway, Donny didn't write the stuff about sex, horny animals on the Nature Channel being close to porn, or the Western Sizzlin' making lovers fart. That was me. Sorry.

Now, I need to apologize to my husband, who was not really paying attention to my asking his blessing to start a blog on his site, even though he managed a little smirkish (is this a word?) smile.

"Dear Donny, sweet husband of enormous compassion. If some people mention that I blogged here last night, I'm so sorry. You said I could, remember, or were you too into that David

Baldacci novel and just said, 'Yes, dear,' like I told you to always say when I asked you something?

"I drank some devil juice called Red Bull, which is a lot like smoking crack, only I don't smoke crack or ever plan to unless something really stressful happens, so don't worry. But that poison in a silver can lead to writing some delightful but off-color stuff on your homepage. Only it wasn't so bad, because a hundred and twenty-four of your friends also friended me, like instantly, and said my musings were much more entertaining than yours, even though you don't use Facebook.

"PS The blog is now removed. I shall create my own blog, as suggested by that friend of yours, who by the way is my new friend now, so the experiment didn't go as bad as you may have been told it did.

"PPS Please tell the county commissioners to look into banning the sale of energy drinks and tearing down that gas trap of a steakhouse. Oh, after I wrote all this blather on your page, something horribly strange happened as I was smashing the Delete key.

"As you know, you told me go ahead and confirm all or your friend requests, so I did, and had no idea a prostitute from the Philippines was one of them.

"She popped in on the 'Chat' feature, because I forgot to turn it off, and she said some icky stuff.

"It started out with, 'Hello sir.' So I typed, 'This is not Donny, but I'm his crazy wife.' So then she wrote, 'Hi Maam (this is her spelling issue not mine). Have a bless afternoon. You want to know me more better? I do nails and love to sucky the toes.'

"She forgot to put the 'ed' on blessed and then asked, 'How are you maam? I hope you still fine. You nice lady and we make fun together. I give you French manicure then you give me French sexy.' That's what she said and how she spelled everything.

"I got nervous about friending her for you, so I wrote, 'I'm fine and also a serial arsonist typing this from prison. I'm also sporting *both* a penis and a vagina, so bye.' I never heard a single peep out of her again.

"PPPS I am done keeping up with your Facebook page and suggest you just sign off for good. I'm afraid I confirmed some unsavory people, maybe even Jerry Sandusky-types or women who star in porno movies. I think the Octomom is one of them."

* Depakote is some kind of acid that is often used to tone down episodes of frenzied or abnormally excited moods. I think it's the antidote of a Red Bull overdose.

Also, when my in-laws read this story, they quit speaking to me. I sent a Hallmark card (well, actually a card from Dollar General), and I haven't heard from them since.

Sometimes when you write some really wild shit, you can lose quality members of the family unit. It's just all part of what we do, sadly. Kind of makes you wish you had said no to drugs.

The Bottom Fish

by Hollis Gillespie

Jesus God, if I need any more evidence—at all—that I am wasting my life, all I have to do is look around at the bunch of bottom fish I have for friends. Grant, for one, wouldn't even pick me up at the airport when I asked him. No, he was busy hanging a chandelier above his dining room table.

"Shut up and get your worthless pansy ass to the airport and pick me up!" I shrieked. "Stop pretending you have a life without me," I said into the empty line. "You'd be nothing without me, you hear that? Nada! Nothing!"

Next I called Lary, which of course was a whole other mind-fuck in futility. He was working. *Lary.* Working. "Oh, my God! You're not supposed to have responsibilities, you retard," I reminded him. "You're supposed to slide through life by sucking on the near-dry teat of public tolerance! Now come get me any-way! They won't miss you for the next hour or so." Lary makes his living rigging things, and unfortunately he was, right then, dangling from a carabiner way high up above stuff and couldn't comfortably extricate himself.

"You douche!" I hollered. "You're nothing without me, got that? Nothing!" Lary, dangling, just laughed, and I could hear the high-uppity-ness in his voice as he told me to eff off.

I would have called Daniel, but he's the one who drove me to the airport to begin with, and you don't want to double-impose on people. He'd left a message earlier to say his mother had called to tell him his father was in the garden shooting armadillos. I really wanted to hear about all the dead armadillos, too, like, can you keep their shells to make lampshades or something, and why does his dad have to shoot them? Can't he just shoo them? But asking a person to make more than one airport run a week is crossing the line. Thank God for Daniel, though. "I'd be nothing without you," I tell him.

Meanwhile, next. I would have called my boyfriend, but he had complained previously that I treated him like he was at my beck and call, so I told him I was sorry and I'd wait for him to call me. But stupidly I'd called him a couple of times after that anyway, and he acted extremely put out by it, so I tried to make up for it with some homemade lasagna, which was a mistake.

First of all, my boyfriend owns a restaurant and is a pretty good cook himself. He can make excellent Thai Panang curry with nothing for utensils except an empty tuna can, a crack lighter, and a fondue fork. So I don't know what I was thinking with the lasagna offering except to say that I usually make fabulous lasagna. But my original recipe calls for all kinds of expensive ingredients you get at uppity markets, like red peppers roasted over a fire of burning gold bullion, sausage made from cows raised on caviar, and cheese aged in bank vaults surrounded by diamonds. In all, one pan load of this stuff costs more than a dinner in Paris, plane ticket and all.

Anyway, lately I've been experiencing what I like to call "income limbo," and I can't afford uppity markets anymore unless it's to go there and troll for food samples, so I've been selecting all my food from the aisle of discounted canned products at the surplus store. I thought I was being quite resourceful, but in truth I guess my improvised lasagna came out tasting like a bowl of old toenails.

That was five weeks ago, and I know it was bad lasagna, but I didn't think it was relationship-wrecking bad. I mean, c'mon.

I've known this guy for a long time; he's seen the worst of me, hasn't he?

Years ago, back when we were just general friends, as opposed to the boy- and girl-variety, he used to sit right across from me at the coffee shop while Grant and I compared torrid car-sex experiences, and let's not forget this man has seen me naked and stuff.

Shit, I keep kicking myself, I should not have made the lasagna. Or maybe I should not have let him see me naked, but it's kind of hard not to be naked when you're naked. Or maybe it was something else. There must be a million things wrong with me, a trillion. In fact, I'm probably just a walking waxball of wrongness, the biggest bottom fish in the trough. Why else would someone you love leave quietly one night and never talk to you again? Not a single word. Nada. Nothing.

I wish I was more like my friend Anna, who is only twenty-seven. I keep comparing myself to her when I was her age, and I always remember that, when I was twenty-seven, I once went on a date with an old flame who'd bragged about how he'd just slept with an interim girlfriend the week before her wedding. I remember making a big show of being sort of quasi-mortified at that, but get this—I was still surprised when he deposited me at my door afterward without so much as making a pass at me.

Anna, I'm thinking, would have been a lot smarter than that. She would not have sat through the entire date with him marveling at how he could use some fellow dude's fiancée like a total toilet seat without throwing something at him, probably. Or at the very least she would have excused herself to use the bathroom and then called a cab at the hostess podium, which is how I sometimes rewrite the story myself when I retell it. Or maybe she would have gotten him to admit his innermost failings right there at the table, had him mewling and curled up like a little bird.

I'm sure she would not have done what I did, which was to expect him to lunge at her at the end of the night and then wonder what her response would have been if he had. God, I hate to even say that.

So I am completely appalled at my twenty-seven-year-old self. I cared about all the wrong crap and I let important people slip from my life and somehow, at the same time, I believed everything. Same as when I was little and I believed my father when he said he wrote the words to "Puff the Magic Dragon," and later believed my mother when our dog Shane disappeared and she said she gave him to—I'm serious—Doris Day. And I would have believed that fiancée-screwing guy if he'd said he was sorry about what he did, like if he'd said he was tortured by his behavior, because most of all, I believed tortured people could be redeemed.

Of course, I ultimately grew the thorny crab shell I keep around my heart, and now I don't even believe my best friend Lary when he says he's been in Chicago working all week. "Like hell!" I hiss into the cell phone. "Shut your lying piehole."

I was hardly past twenty-seven when I first met Lary, but we can't blame him for my hard fall into pragmatism. If anything, he's been trying to float my fantasies all this time, filling my head with all kinds of castles in the sky.

"So you sold your soul," he comforted me once, draping his arm across my shoulders, "It'll grow back. There's plenty to go around." Ha. I wished I could believe him. Sometimes I think about that guy, my former five-night stand (about) who slept with his ex-girlfriend right before she married someone else, how he boasted about it. I believed everything, including him when he said he had no feelings for her "what-so-fucking-ever."

"What were you doing there then?" I asked, but he didn't answer. He just ushered me home. It was raining, and he seemed to stare at the wet highway like it could lead him to the past, like maybe back to that night when he had her in his arms and could have turned away but made the mistake of staying, or perhaps even earlier, when he could have kept her with him but made the mistake of leaving.

Does your soul really grow back, I wonder? Because sometimes, when I think of that night, I find myself seeing some torture in his eyes as he gazed at the highway. I find myself hoping he went right back to her that night and took her in his arms and never let her go. God, I hate to even say that.

***

All right, so how long do you have to wait for your boyfriend to call before he becomes your ex-boyfriend? In answer to that, I'd say that two weeks with no call is definitely evidence that the relationship is over, but your state of denial over your discarded status is proportionate to the feelings you have for the person who discarded you, so I gave him eight weeks. Eight weeks before I finally I decided that just because Keiger and I weren't dating anymore didn't mean I couldn't continue to go to the restaurant he runs and continue to act like I owned the place. So I went there a few nights ago and told all the customers that everything was on the house. I really enjoyed doing that. People were so grateful to me. So I returned yesterday.

"Everything's on the house," I kept hollering, but the only person to hear me was Grant, who works there. The bar was empty but it was early yet. I'd called beforehand to warn Keiger I was coming in. "I'll be there in a few minutes, so if you're gonna leave like last time, do it now, because I don't want you humiliating me by running out the back door the second I show up." Like getting dumped isn't humiliating enough. To Keiger's credit, though, he did not leave when I got there. Instead he stayed put and complained that in the two months since we'd talked I could have called him.

"What kind of relationship is it if I have to call you all the time?" he asked, evidently forgetting the moratorium on my calling him he'd put in place.

"Keiger, you don't have to call me all the time," I informed him, "but you do have to call me more than never again." *Jesus God*, I really wonder how some people get through the day without someone else pounding a stake through their head. Just for chuckles, I exclaimed, "So if you didn't dump me, and I didn't dump you, then I guess we're still together, huh?" but I was less prepared for the panic in his face than I thought I'd be.

Love is love. I know it when I see it.

Hollis Gillespie is an award-winning humor and travel columnist, with her column appearing every month on Atlanta Magazine's *coveted back page. She is also a best-selling memoirist, NPR commentator, professional speaker, comedian, and guest on the* Tonight Show with Jay Leno. *She has been featured on scores of TV shows and blogs and runs Shocking Real Life, the largest writing school in Atlanta, which offers workshops on blogging and social media. She is the author of* Bleachy-Haired Honky Bitch: Tales from a Bad Neighborhood, Confessions of a Recovering Slut and Other Love Stories, *and* Trailer Trashed; My Dubious Efforts Toward Upward Mobility. *Two of her books have been optioned for television. These days she gets most of her exercise running to catch flights. Contact Hollis through* www.ShockingRealLife.com.

That Thing at the End of a Sentence

by Jen Mann-Li

In 1993, I was a junior in college. I was studying abroad that summer in Ukraine. In those days Ukraine had very few of the comforts of home (this was the early nineties; McDonald's hadn't even arrived yet). I had been warned to pack essentials like toilet paper and toothpaste and most importantly, tampons. Being the good do-bee that I am, I took an entire suitcase of t.p., Crest, and Tampax. My roommate had ignored that part of the list and came ill prepared. Practically on day one, "It" came with a vengeance. You know what I'm talking about: the thing that comes at the end of a sentence came to visit and she was freaking out. I told her she could use some of my supplies until we found a drugstore and then she could get some of her own. I had no idea what a production that would be.

Every day on our way to class we had a side mission, searching for a place to purchase tampons. We couldn't find that familiar blue box. We couldn't even find Playtex or o.b. Nothing! Then we started to wonder. Maybe Ukrainian women didn't use tampons. Maybe they used sanitary napkins. So we started looking for sanitary napkins (the horror, but they would have to do).

179

Finally we just hoped to find some clean rags she could stuff in her pants. My roomie continued to bleed like a fucking stuck pig and she ran through my entire supply. Great. Now my visit was due and I was up shit creek.

In the meantime, I had a met a cute boy, Ivan. I was too busy flirting awkwardly with Ivan to focus on the pressing need that was coming in fourteen short days. Every time he took me out, I'd ask him to show me different types of stores. He wanted to know what kind of store I was looking for. I started with asking for a pharmacy. He took me to a small, dark space with shelves lined with bottles of medicine I couldn't read, bandages, and booze. They did not have what I needed. Next, I asked for a grocery store. Not even close—a few hunks of bread, some mystery meat, and Coca-Cola was all those shelves held. I inquired about a "woman's store." Of course Ivan did not know what the fuck I was talking about. "What is a woman's store?" he asked.

"Y'know…they have things for women…"

"Do they have these stores in America?"

"Kinda…" I replied. At twenty-one, I was entirely too embarrassed to tell this guy what I was looking for. This was a guy I was attracted to; I didn't want him to think about me bleeding. I wanted him to think about me naked!

Every time we went out, I would run into any random store I saw that I had not been in already. He must have thought I had some kind of shopping addiction. Did you know they had entire department stores full of nothing but orange down jackets? All sizes. But only in orange. I considered buying one and tearing it apart and fashioning my own DIY feminine care products with the down lining.

But still no fucking tampons.

Finally, it was almost D-day and the panic was setting in. I didn't know what I was going to do. By the way I was acting, you would have thought I was actually knocked up.

Obviously Ivan could feel my anxiety. Finally, he sat me down and said in his thick Russian accent, "Jen, tell me what you are looking for. I can help you find it."

I was still too embarrassed to tell him what I needed. I refused.

"Jen, it is upsetting you and I want to help you. Is it a special souvenir you would like?"

A souvenir? Ha! Not even close.

The night before my crimson tide was scheduled to roll in, I became desperate. After a few shots of homemade vodka I broke down and told him what I needed. While Ivan's English was excellent, he'd been taught by a very prim and proper British professor who had never really taken it upon himself to teach his coed class the word "tampon." It only took an English-to-Russian dictionary, a little bit of charades, and finally a hand-drawn picture of various Kotex/o.b./Tampax boxes for Ivan to get the message (and blush as soon as he did).

"Do you know where I can find these?" I asked hopefully.

"Yes," he replied, "but it will be expensive. You can only get them on the black market."

"I don't care. I'll pay. I have dollars. How much to get them tonight?"

"I do not know. Maybe twenty?" he said.

"For a box?" I said incredulously. Fuck it, who cared? That roommate was going to pay! "Fine. Whatever. Just get them, please." We arranged for him to go and see what he could find on the "black market" (I actually thought it was an actual market and asked if I could go and do some shopping) and then meet later that night at a party.

I got to the party before him. I was hanging with my new cool European friends when he walked in with a plastic bag. Ivan came up to and said very formally, "I have a gift for you."

"Great. Thanks. I owe ya," I said and I tried to swipe the bag from him before everyone could see what he had.

"No, Jen," he said pulling the bag out of my reach. "In this country, gifts are very special. You must be presented just right or else the gift is spoiled."

"I don't want a gift. I will pay you for them," I hissed.

"No. I insist. You will be leaving at the end of the summer and I have not bought you anything to remember me by," Ivan said. "I want to give you this as a gift."

Remember you by? Are you kidding me? They're tampons. I'm not going to save one to remember you by. I thought to myself.

Now everyone was gathering around to see what amazing gift my new cute friend was going to give me to remember him by.

I was dying inside. "Please don't, Ivan," I whispered. I wanted a hole to open right then and swallow me.

He made a huge production of pulling out a giant box of Tampax. "Ooooh," a few Ukrainian girls said.

"I present this gift of Tampax to you. It is my pleasure to give you this gift," said Ivan looking deep into my eyes and smiling kindly at me. "I got you the big box. I did not know how many you would need. You are a big girl, I thought you might have a big menses."

He was absolutely right. I never forgot him. His gift was one of the most memorable I've ever received. Every time I look at a box of Tampax I think of Ivan.

Jen is the anonymous blogger throwing hilarious punches peppered with a liberal dose of f-bombs on her blog www.peopleiwanttopunchinthethroat.com. Yeah, the name pretty much sums it up. It ain't called Rainbows & Unicorns, people, so tread lightly and watch yourself in the comments section—knife fights have been known to break out occasionally. Jen's 51,000+ fans on Facebook are constantly accusing her of saying what everyone else is just thinking. No one is safe from her ire. She's gone after innocent elves on shelves, douchey dads, placenta-eating movie stars, and annoying parents. Her sarcastic, irreverent, snarky, and polarizing blog averages one million hits a month.

Jen hasn't got a book or a newspaper column that you can read—apparently she's allergic to ink. She has been featured on HuffingtonPost. com and Babble.com. (That's almost like having a syndicated column in a hundred newspapers around the country or a book on Amazon, right?)

The various awards that she's received include such keepers as honoree for the BlogHer 2012 Voice of the Year, first place in the Circle of Moms Top 25 Funniest Mom Blogs and Cutest Blog Award (this one was sent to her accidentally and has since been rescinded; her blog looks like shit).

Personality Profile Q&A

by Ben Baker

Personality and relationship profile articles are one of the main features in women's magazines. Not since the 1970s has a men's magazine featured a "real" Q&A profile article.

After spending a week of research reviewing lingerie ads in women's magazines and every now and then looking at the "profiles" article and studiously poring over hundreds of back issues of *Penthouse* magazine, I have put together a "profile" questionnaire suitable for every member of the family, even your weird brother…

Just choose an answer from the multiple choice answers.

1) Your idea of a perfect evening is:
a. A quiet romantic dinner for two, dancing, and so forth.
b. Peace and quiet.
c. An all-night Barney marathon.
   d. Cool movie and no curfew.
   e. A 12-pack, some viennies, some poles, and a pond or river bank.
   f. In bed by eight p.m.

g. Whips, chains, steel spikes, and someone who screams really well.

2) Your idea of a perfect meal is:
   a. Anything by candlelight.
   b. Anything that doesn't wind up on the floor, walls, ceiling or in the dog.
   c. Mac & cheese, burgers and fries.
   d. A buffet.
   e. A 12-pack, some viennies, some poles, and a pond or river bank.
   f. Anything easy to digest.
   g. Served on a quivering torso.

3) Your dream vacation is:
   a. Tahiti, Cozumel, Acapulco, or Bermuda.
   b. A weekend with NOTHING to do.
   c. Any place with giant cartoon characters come to life.
   d. Panama City Beach.
   e. A 12-pack, some viennies, some poles, and a pond or river bank.
   f. Somewhere warm with low humidity.
   g. A visit to the San Francisco SM/BD scene.

4) Your ideal significant other is someone who:
   a. Enjoys moonlight walks on the beach and poetry.
   b. Can handle high-pitched screams, constant yelling, and bodily fluids without going ballastic.
   c. Doesn't eat your crayons.
   d. Has a driver's license.
   e. Has a 12-pack, some viennies, some poles, and a pond or river bank.
   f. Can drive at night.
   g. Has no safe word.

5) When looking for a long-term relationship, the most important thing is:
   a. Commitment.
   b. Everything in a large, economy size.

c. Shares the juice cup.

d. Has own vehicle.

e. A 12-pack, some viennies, some poles, and a pond or river bank.

f. Number of joint replacements.

g. Soundproofed room.

6. If given $1 million, you would:

a. Promote world peace, help the homeless, etc.

b. Buy a bigger version of everything.

c. Party all night.

e. Buy 12-pack—heck, a case—some viennies, some poles, and a pond or river bank.

f. Buy a turbocharged pacemaker.

g. Build that ceiling-suspended four-way stretching rack with optional electrocution switches.

7. Your favorite clothes are:

a. An evening dress or slacks and a smoking jacket with a silk cravat.

b. Easy to get stains out of.

c. "Favorite" as in clothes? You gotta be kidding.

d. Jeans, loose fitting shirt, the latest sneakers.

e. A 12-pack, some viennies, some poles, and a pond or river bank.

f. Polyester.

g. Leather & latex.

8. You would prefer to see:

a. An opera.

b. The back of your eyelids for twelve uninterrupted hours.

c. Sesame Street on Ice.

d. Lollapalooza.

e. A 12-pack, some viennies, some poles, and a pond or river bank.

f. Next week.

g. To a depth of about twelve inches inside a person through any of several body cavities.

9. Your most recent significant achievement is:
   a. Reading the entire works of Sidney Sheldon.
   b. Getting out of bed.
   c. A B C D E F G...
   d. Successfully using a fake ID.
   e. A 12-pack, some viennies, some poles, and a pond or river bank.
   f. This morning's trip to the bathroom.
   g. Full insertion of a fourteen-inch long, three-inch diameter dildo into that slut's ass.

10. When going somewhere you take:
    a. A portable Neiman Marcus department store.
    b. The entire contents of the house.
    c. A suitcase full of Barbie dolls, the entire G.I. Joe set, and things that shoot plastic projectiles or water.
    d. Money and/or credit cards.
    e. A 12-pack, some viennies, some poles, and a pond or river bank.
    f. A pharmacy.
    g. A riding crop.

11) If you could vote for anyone for president, it would be:
    a. Hillary Clinton.
    b. Bill Cosby.
    c. Elmo.
    d. Aerosmith.
    e. A 12-pack, some viennies, some poles, and a pond or river bank.
    f. Ronald Reagan.
    g. The Marquis de Sade.

12) The most important thing to you is:
    a. A good complexion.
    b. Restraining the urge to strangle.
    c. Blue's Clues.
    d. Nothing is important.
    e. A 12-pack, some viennies, some poles, and a pond or river bank.

f. Living long enough to be a burden.

g. A really satisfying scream.

13) Your next major goal in life is:

a. A complete facial.

b. Graduation.

c. Extracting revenge from sibling.

d. Graduation.

e. A 12-pack, some viennies, some poles, and a pond or river bank.

f. An afternoon nap.

g. A fifteen-inch long, three and a half-inch diameter dildo fully inserted in that slut's ass.

14) Your most recent major investment was:

a. A week-long stay at a health spa.

b. Groceries.

c. What's an investment?

d. A tank of gas.

e. A 12-pack, some viennies, some poles, and a pond or river bank.

f. A six-week newspaper subscription.

g. Wall-mounted cross with breathing-control device.

15) You are most concerned about:

a. Wrinkles.

b. Permanent damage.

c. Finding Waldo.

d. A reason for anything.

e. A 12-pack, some viennies, some poles, and a pond or river bank.

f. Falling.

g. Whether to use a cat-o-nine tails, a bull whip, a cattle prod, or all three.

Give yourself 1 point for each a., 2 for each b., 3 for each c., 4 for each d., 5 for each e., 6 for each f., and 7 for each g.

If you didn't bother to take this test, you certainly shouldn't be reading the carefully developed and incredibly accurate results.

If you scored 15, you are mentally unstable and have no friends. You should get out of your house and see what life actually is.

If you scored 30, uh, Mom, why did you take this test? If you're not Mom, you need help. You need lots of help. May we humbly suggest several full-time assistants?

If you scored 45, you are a very cool, likeable, and all-around well-adjusted person. You are not perfect, but you freely admit that someone else did it.

If you scored 60, you are depressed, sullen, and very annoying to be around. Fortunately, this will only last a few years, after which you will return to the old depressed, sullen, and very annoying person those around you have come to hate.

If you scored 75, you are as close to perfect as a human being can be on this planet. Everyone around you wishes they could be just like you.

If you scored 90, you are a poster child for euthansia. Die and make room for younger people.

If you scored 105, you are a sick bitch. Can I have your phone number?

If you scored anything other than the above scores, you must have taken the test incorrectly. In other words, you failed. You will have to repeat the class to earn credit.

Ben Baker is the Redneck Genius. His syndicated humor column probably doesn't appear in your local newspaper, but you can read it each week at www.irock109.com/wiregrass.php . *He's received more than one hundred awards for work in communications and a few of them actually belonged to him. He dispenses cheap wisdom and drinks expensive bourbon and moderately priced beer from his farm in south Georgia. He is the author of several books that are used to stun laboratory mice prior to their being used in surgical experiments. You can reach him at GodOfHumor@Southernhumorists.com.*

Warm Cinnamon Buns

by Charles Dowdy

One stupid book and I'm standing in the middle of my kitchen, naked, making cinnamon rolls.

The book was one of those gifts we received at a sex wedding shower. The invitation didn't read like that—it was called a bedroom party or something like that. The obnoxious people we called friends thought that meant this was a contest to see who could buy the largest battery operated sexual apparatus. I remember because this was the same party where I got the edible chocolate underwear that melted all over my crotch while my wife was "freshening up" in the bathroom.

The book was called *101 Ways to Spice up your Marriage in 101 Days*. The spine of the book creaked as my wife opened it, which might not have been a good sign.

"There are no pictures," my wife said. "Watch the road."

"You're lying. What's that?"

"Stick figure sex? You're going to drive your family into a grove of pine trees so you can see some stick figures having sex?"

Anyway, the format of the book is that each of the 101 spicy ideas is sealed in a pouch and you have to select which number you want and then tear it out. Needless to say, you don't know what you're getting into, but the names can provide some direction. There was "Angel with a Lariat," "The Thrill of the Chase around the Couch," "Mustang Sally," and my personal favorite, "Halftime Shenanigans." That title alone should have set off all kinds of alarms about the practicality of this book. I can just hear myself panting, "We've got to get this thing done, honey; I can hear Madden in there."

My wife had decided to flip through the book on a trip back from her parents' house. One second she's reading some celebrity rag and sympathizing with Brad and Angie, and then all of a sudden she whips out the sex book. I don't know where she found it. She had been giving me a hard time about the regularity of our sex life, to which I would point out that if it hadn't been so regular before, we wouldn't have the four mouths to feed that were dominating our life and we might have a chance for a little alone time. Maybe my wife thought the book was supposed to be research. With the kids in the back of the car it struck me as bad timing, but suddenly she decides she's the Jacques Cousteau of sexual exploration. The kids were immersed in some video that pretty much guaranteed them a life of petty crime as my wife started whispering some of the more risqué titles.

I have to admit I got a little nervous. I wasn't sure I was up to this. Of course, my wife wasn't exactly wild about all of the suggestions either; she would have, in fact, slapped my face had I suggested some of this stuff before she saw it in this book. But here she is now offended because I'm not getting real excited about the one called "The Pizza Man Always Rings Twice," which calls for quite the talent since he apparently has his hands preoccupied with the pizza boxes. I'm not sure I'm willing to touch our doorbell with that part of my body, if I'm even capable.

Nope, ensconced in the safety of our automobile, where it was going to be kind of hard to play out something called "The Tender Outlaw," my wife insisted I choose a number.

I tried to play it off. What if I got something really freaky that I didn't want to do? How would she react to a do-over? But my wife wouldn't let go of it. She acted more and more offended the longer this went on. For the next forty miles she harassed me about it until I finally snapped.

"Fine, damn it. What did you say number seventy-six was?"

"Epicurean Delight."

"I'll take that one."

"How original. I should have known you'd choose something to do with food."

She threw the spicy package at me. I jammed it in my pocket and endured her pouting for the rest of the afternoon.

After we got home, she left for the grocery store without a word. So I pulled out the package from the car and started reading.

And that's how I ended up in a face-off in the kitchen with my wife at five thirty the next morning.

A reasonable person would guess that my wife came into the kitchen first thing because she smelled cinnamon rolls and she was hungry. But according to the package from the book, I was supposed to position myself between my wife and her morning coffee.

Custer had a better plan.

"What the hell are you doing?" my wife demanded as she went to the cabinet for a coffee cup.

"Making breakfast for you," I said.

"Did you forget something?"

I thought back to my instructions. No, it was all here.

"Like what?"

"Clothes."

"Don't start with me. This was your idea." I grabbed the folded "spice" package off the counter and started reading it aloud for her. "Your wife will wake to the smell of something delicious cooking. She'll be grinning by the time she reaches the kitchen. Then she'll see that it seems you've managed to get flour everywhere: in your hair, all over the counters, and on the dogs."

She had her hands on her hips. "Where's the flour?"

"What?"

"In your hair? On the dogs? Where's the flour?"

"I didn't want you to get mad about the mess so I went with premade cinnamon rolls."

"You skipped the flour?"

"Like flour is real sexy. Like you've always wanted to roll around in flour and then have sex. And, according to the genius who wrote this book, now I'm supposed to lean in to kiss my wife good morning, but instead of kissing her I will wipe a big dab of cinnamon on her cheek."

"Huh," was all she said as she reached for the coffeepot.

"So," I said as I leaned in to kiss her.

"You wipe that damn cinnamon on me and I'll knee those boys into the middle of next week."

Undeterred, I reached out to dab some cinnamon on her cheek, just like the book told me to. She slapped my hand.

"Look. You insisted we do this. The book says I'm supposed to smear some cinnamon on your cheek."

"Fine," she said. "Wipe the damn cinnamon on me."

So I did.

Then she said, "Is this foreplay or are you trying to make me look like an edible Pocahontas?"

"That's nothing. Now we're supposed to have sex on the kitchen table."

My wife started to laugh.

"I didn't make this stuff up. Look!"

"I'm supposed to meet the girls to run in five minutes. I've already got to wash my face, climbing onto the breakfast table is not an option."

One of the four-year-old twins had wandered into the kitchen, his blankie spread over his head so that he looked like a two-foot Moses.

"Why is Daddy naked?"

"Good question," my wife said as she poured a cup of coffee.

"Because Mom is not satisfied with our sex life and she brought some moron into our bedroom."

"What's a moron?" the twin asked.

"The guy I married," my wife said as she disappeared to go wash her face. I grabbed a robe out of the laundry room before any of the other kids woke up. As I made breakfast for the mob, I couldn't help focusing on that robe.

I decided that married sex is kind of like a robe you've had a long time. It's comfortable, you like it, and you don't want to let go of it. Sure, there might be a few holes, it may be a tad threadbare, and now it comes up over your knees. But it feels better than ever.

Still, that doesn't mean you're pulling a Hugh Hefner and wearing that robe in public anymore.

I decided whoever wrote that book had no idea what they were talking about and obviously had no kids. Cinnamon and sex in the kitchen before breakfast? The whole idea was ludicrous. I mean, what's a responsible father supposed to say to a four-year-old who's crying because he's got nowhere to eat his breakfast and his roll doesn't have any cinnamon on it?

"Oh, that's all right, buddy, there's still plenty of cinnamon left on your mom's face."

Charles Dowdy is a broadcaster living in Louisiana. He is husband to one, father to four, and the morning show host on WYLK The Lake, where he has learned to deftly navigate from the sponsored obituary report (the list of who kicked off overnight) to songs like "Moves Like Jagger" by Maroon 5. His book, I Wear the Shorts in this Family, *is available on Amazon.*

For the Love of Dog

by Lisa K. Nelson

O n the fourth night of my family vacation (oxymoron alert) out west, I had a dream about my dog and, well, I'm not sure how to put this: I was kinda sorta making out with my dog. Mind you, this was first base only—no tongue (at least not mine)—but there was heavy petting, if you will.

This would not surprise the majority of my friends or family.

"You love Sandy more than us," is a familiar complaint from my three kids. My immediate response is "duh," and sometimes it even slips out audibly. I can't help it. I mean, everybody talks about it, but you cannot say it enough: Unconditional love—dogs just do it better than any other living creature. Paws down.

Dogs are givers. Children are takers. Why do you think there are no "seeing-eye kids"? Imagine that poor blind sap, ditched for dead at first sight of an ice cream truck or lightning bug. Also, dogs come when you call them, and obedience school and discipline actually work with them. There is no greater satisfaction for a mother than to have somebody—anybody—even a different species—actually *listen* to her. And then to take it a step further and actually *do* the thing you've asked?

Oh... my... sweet... lord. Even if it's just dropping a saliva-soaked tennis ball at your feet, at this point in my life, that ranks right up there with great sex. (With a human. I swear.)

What about your husband, some of you might be asking? And that would be the "some of you" out there who don't have one. Let me throw a couple stats out there: According to the Internet shopping site Shopzilla, 56 percent of women pet owners surveyed felt their pets were more affectionate than their partners, and 45 percent said their pets were cuter. Another poll proclaimed that 33 percent of women felt their pets were better listeners than their husbands.

My only reaction to that (after "duh") is that the numbers seem quite low. Perhaps that's just the "cat factor."

As for my husband, the cute competition is not a fair one (even Channing Tatum would struggle versus a mini golden doodle). But my dog is definitely more empathetic than my partner—and instinctually so. She is the first to notice when I am sad or sick, and she always knows the right thing to say—you got it, nothing.

My husband, on the other hand, operates in a spectrum that stems from ignoring to dismissing to outright blaming me for whatever malady I have. "Well, whose fault is that?" is his go-to phrase. For example, if I am in the bathroom retching just this side of the white tunnel of dead relatives, he will come at me with, "Well, you ordered the Applebee's mussel wrap. Whose fault is that?"

But I'm not here to trash men (not this time anyway), but rather to canonize canines. I'd do anything for Sandy, and she'd do more for me. We live in this blissful mutual adoration society the likes of which I never thought possible.

A couple of confessions:

Most mornings when I wake up, I am absolutely giddy to find Sandy's scruffy chin propped on my shoulder instead of my husband's. I'm a sucker for the adoring gaze and wagging tail instead of...well, you know...other appendages wagging.

And once when I was walking Sandy as a puppy, my five-year-old following on his bike, I rushed to *her* side first when we all collided while the fruit of my loins flailed about, knees bloodied, on the ground.

And as for the exact replica paw-print tattoo: it's not a question of if but where.

Which all begs the question (if you will): Am I too close to my dog? Have I turned into Betty White, or worse yet, my wacky neighbor in L.A. who loved animals more than humans and once resuscitated a squirrel that fell into her pool?

I did read about a woman in England who actually breastfed her puppy, which, rest assured, I absolutely find sick and twisted. So, I guess as long as she's out there, I'm OK.

Right?

Like everything, my extreme attachment to this animal probably stems from my childhood. I wanted a dog more than anything as a kid. I had no siblings and two Scandinavian parents, which is a bit like being raised by wolves—without the playfulness. I craved cuddly. After years of begging, I had to settle for a fairly realistic-looking (I'll give it that) Steiff stuffed schnauzer that I dragged around the block on a leash.

"Did she really skip a grade?" "She doesn't seem quite right." "This is what all that organic food leads to." I imagine this was the buzz as I passed by.

I did actually have a living, breathing pet once. A crayfish— perhaps the most homely and least hardy of all animals. Craig didn't even make it through the night after being plucked from a creek in Wisconsin, overwhelmed and confused, I imagine, by all the dollhouse furniture floating in his tank.

So I guess my dear, sweet, sainted Sandy is much more than just a dog to me. She represents lost childhood hopes and dreams sprung to life. A knight in shining fur. The ultimate rescue animal.

So what if the best relationship I have going is just this side of lesbian bestiality.

It's all good, clean fun.

And at least she isn't stuffed.

Yet.

Lisa K. Nelson has been a working writer since graduating with a journalism degree from the University of Illinois. Realizing quickly that news writing was not for someone who liked to make things up, she switched to advertising and became quite proficient. Prone to extreme impulsivity and disdain for all things safe and secure, she was propelled by one sketch writing class at Chicago's The Second City to Hollywood to write for situation comedies such as Everybody Loves Raymond, Suddenly Susan, *and* Ellen. *The following decade, Lisa moved back to Chicago—dedicating herself to raising her three children, who quickly grew into ungrateful urchins who kvetched endlessly about her not staying in Hollywood and making more money.*

An award-winning columnist, blogger, and podcaster, Lisa is headed back to Hollywood in 2012 to write for the Disney Channel sitcom Crash and Bernstein, *where she will once again be paid for blurting inappropriate comments—a tendency that has received mixed reviews in midwestern suburbia.*

Susan Reinhardt *is the author of the* Amazon *and* Malaprop's *bookstore top seller, in its seventh printing,* Not Tonight Honey, Wait 'Til I'm a Size Six *(Kensington, 2005) and* Don't Sleep with a Bubba *(Kensington, 2007), winner of a* January Magazine Book of the Year *award.* Dishing with the Kitchen Virgin, *a culinary bestseller, came out in May 2008,.*

Many of her stories have been anthologized in the best-selling More Sand in My Bra *series (May 2007), featuring heavy hitters like Laurie Notaro and Ellen DeGeneres, and she has a story in* Southern Fried Farce, *which features authors such as Roy Blount, Jr. and Celia Rivenbark. She was one of twelve authors chosen to write the serial novel* Naked Came the Leaf Peeper, *also a Malaprop's best seller.*

Reinhardt is a syndicated columnist with Gannett Newspapers, the largest chain in the country, and her work has appeared in magazines and newspapers worldwide, including The Washington Post, where she has a syndicated piece.

She has won dozens of national awards, including Gannett's Outstanding Writer of the Year, and for twelve consecutive years she was named best columnist in western North Carolina.

Reinhardt stars in videos for the newspaper, some which have gone viral. Have you seen her Sarah Palin impression? Hundreds of thousands have!

She has also delivered hundreds of speeches, including the keynote address—along with Dave Barry—at the Erma Bombeck Writer's Conference.

Her column appears in countless newspapers across the country each week, reaching more than one million readers. She is also a regular guest on radio stations across the country and has been featured in More *magazine and appeared on the* Today Show. *Reinhardt is the mother of two, and for kicks, she rides a unicycle and twirls a baton—at the same time. She loves doing stand-up comedy and performs for charities.*

DC Stanfa *is the author of* The Art of Table Dancing: Escapades of an Irreverent Woman *(Orange Frazer Press), which was recognized as one of the top ten memoirs at the New York Book Festival in June 2007. It was published internationally by Librario.*

After a couple of decades selling empty boxes for a living, Stanfa embarked on a second tree-killing profession (and finally put that PR/ journalism degree to some use) as a writer.

She has made various television appearances and was featured in an interview for In The Tank, *a documentary program on PBS. Stanfa has appeared in several publications, including* The Cincinnati Enquirer *and* Ohio Magazine, *and has appeared several times in* Susan Reinhardt's *column. She also contributed a story and a parody diet to Reinhardt's* Dishing with the Kitchen Virgin.

Stanfa was a regularly featured guest/book reviewer on Cincinnati radio station Q102's website Amy's Table: A Girl's Guide to Living, *for a segment called "Two Books and a Beach."*

Hosting dozens of beach party book signings, this beach fanatic traipsed from the Midwest to Caribbean and Atlantic Coast beaches. Her trademarked phrase, **Will Dance For Margaritas**™, *adorns hats and other promotional items, and is also the title of her forthcoming book. Stanfa mentors women in both business and the arts. She has also been on faculty at several writers' conferences, teaching humor writing workshops.*

She has a real diamond but is only fake-engaged to her pool boy/retired police chief/bodyguard boyfriend. Her website is www.dcstanfa.com.

Made in the USA
Lexington, KY
17 February 2013